Unveiled

Poetic Reflections
of
A Yielding Heart

BY JENNY MATHEWS

Balboa Press books may be ordered through booksellers or by contacting:

Balboa Press
A Division of Hay House
1663 Liberty Drive
Bloomington, IN 47403
www.balboapress.com
1 (877) 407-4847

Cover and Illustrations Artwork By: Suzy Schultz

ISBN: 978-1-9822-2916-0 (sc)
ISBN: 978-1-9822-2915-3 (e)

Library of Congress Control Number: 2019906771

Printed in China.

Balboa Press rev. date: 08/13/2019

BALBOA
PRESS
A DIVISION OF HAY HOUSE

DEDICATION

to
Dwight
beloved husband, amazing father, faithful friend

to
Julie and Rich
our wonderful children

and to
their awesome families
Ray, Cole, Jocelyn, Will, Grant, and Lizzy

foremost to
The Holy Spirit of God
without Whose inspiration, this book would not exist

INTRODUCTION

I yielded my life to Christ at age thirty when I asked Him to send His Holy Spirit to guide me. His Word (the Holy Bible) became alive and I felt as if I were on a honeymoon with Jesus. As I began meditating in the Word, I would receive a "prompting" and the words I wrote came to me in poetic form. I never studied poetry, but, the poems kept coming, and I began to greatly look forward to my time alone with my Lord to hear what He had to say. Jesus revealed Himself to me, not only as my Savior, but my defender, my refuge, my sustainer, my best friend, my Lord and the lover of my soul.

During the time I was writing these poems, life was good. They weren't all born out of my experiences, but mostly out of revelation from the Holy Spirit. I suppose it was my way of journaling. I know this...during the time spent writing these poems, I felt like I was in the sweet presence of God.

Later in my life, I began to experience the pain of different trials...taking care of my aging parents, and, worst of all, taking care of my husband of forty five years through a bone marrow transplant and his subsequent death. I felt I was living out these poems; and, believe me, there were many that I didn't want to experience. My whole world was shaken and my faith was tested.

Then the words that I had written through the years began to speak to me to convict, comfort and point me once again to God's great love in Christ. I have found the grace to sustain me as I continue my journey through life even in the face of a diagnosis of ALS in the year 2018. Jesus said, "Peace I leave with you; My [own] peace I now give and bequeath to you. Do not let your heart be troubled, neither let it be afraid." I am living in His gift of peace.

This book of poems reflects my journey of forty years. Come along with me...from the first whisper of Jesus to follow Him, through valleys deep and mountain peaks to our forever home. Discover the extreme love of our Heavenly Father leading to the sacrifice of His Son for the forgiveness of our sins; and the gift of the Holy Spirit sent into the hearts of His children to guide, strengthen, comfort, empower and make anew.

Discover that God is for us!

Step into His love...

~ J M ~

"We all, with unveiled face beholding as in a mirror the glory of the Lord, are being transformed into the same image from glory to glory, just as from the Lord, the Spirit."

II CORINTHIANS 3:18

Unveil my heart.

Reveal the mystery...

Let me Your glory see

In the face of Jesus Christ.

Unveil my heart.

Reveal Your love to me...

The love of Calvary...

Love's sacrifice.

~ J M ~

Unveiled

TABLE OF CONTENTS

I

THE WHISPER OF GOD

Be still and know that I am God.

PSALM 46:10

Be Still

Be still, my heart and listen.

Your Maker longs for you.

In quietness, His whispers

of love will filter through.

Beyond the veil, He beckons,

"Come, My dear one, come."

Eternal Life, the second

you make His heart your home.

To know Him is to cherish

His loving sacrifice.

Come now, embrace the promise

secured for you in Christ.

Be still...be still...be still.

Follow Me

"Follow me." He says, so gently;
and again, "Come, follow Me.
And I will show you wondrous things
of life eternally.

Follow Me where e'er I lead you
though the road be hard and rough.
Follow Me into the darkness
for My Light will be enough..

to guide you through each pathway,
each storm upon the sea.
My grace will be sufficient.
Just come, come follow Me."

So I yielded to His beckon ~
took those first steps cautiously.
My mind cried out, "I'm frightened",
for the end I could not see.

But still He beckoned gently,
and I found to my surprise,
if I would only trust Him,
He would open up my eyes..

to see each step before me ~
not the full path for you see,
I may not yet be ready
to embrace His plans for me.

So my Savior, in His gracious way,
goes step by step with me.
And I have learned 'tis better far
to walk thus patiently..

to leave to Him the future
to reveal when He can see
a heart fully surrendered to
His words, "Come, follow Me."

Be Still and Know

Though you do not see My hand,

I am working.

Though you do not hear My voice,

I still speak.

My promise is the source of all rejoicing.

Praise brings down My power

For the weak.

Though you do not feel Me near,

I am present.

Though you cannot see My eyes,

I gaze on you.

My streams run ever cool in the desert.

Believe. Receive My grace

To see you through.

Though you do not know My heart,

I am your heartbeat.

Though you cannot feel My breath,

I breathe in you.

My Life I gave that I might draw you to Me.

Be still and know. My love

for you is true.

Flight

Take flight, My child. Arise, take flight.

Upon My golden wings be borne

to places far beyond your sight.

We'll catch sunrays before the morn.

You'll see the stars fall from My hand

and watch Me set the moon in place.

Heaven's door at My command

will open with a flood of grace.

Above the mountains we will soar,

then to the vale in quick descent

where liberty makes its implore

and healing streams lend their consent.

Then off to ever loftier heights

until that final joyous flight

Oasis

Come, my child, unto My fount;

I give Myself for thee.

My thoughts of you ~ too vast to count.

Oh, come, come unto Me.

Drink, with joy, My waters pure;

look only unto Me.

My strength will cause you to endure.

I am all you need.

Rest upon My sea of love;

look not to either shore.

Stay your mind on Me above;

be quenched forevermore.

I, for you, am everything;

away with Me, elope.

Within your desert, I now bring

oasis of your hope.

Sweet Solitude

In quietness, I come before Your throne

to seek to know You ~ just Your voice to hear.

Awaiting, all my thoughts on You alone.

Oh, Savior, bid me come. Draw me near.

The blanket of Your presence comforts me,

enveloping, then reaching deep inside.

Within this place, serene security

is mine to have, to hold as I abide.

Sweet solitude ~ this time I gladly give

to bask within the warmth of Your embrace.

Sustain me, Lord, for I long to live

imbibing from Your loving cup of grace.

A world awaits without; and now I go,

refreshed, in awe once more that You, I know.

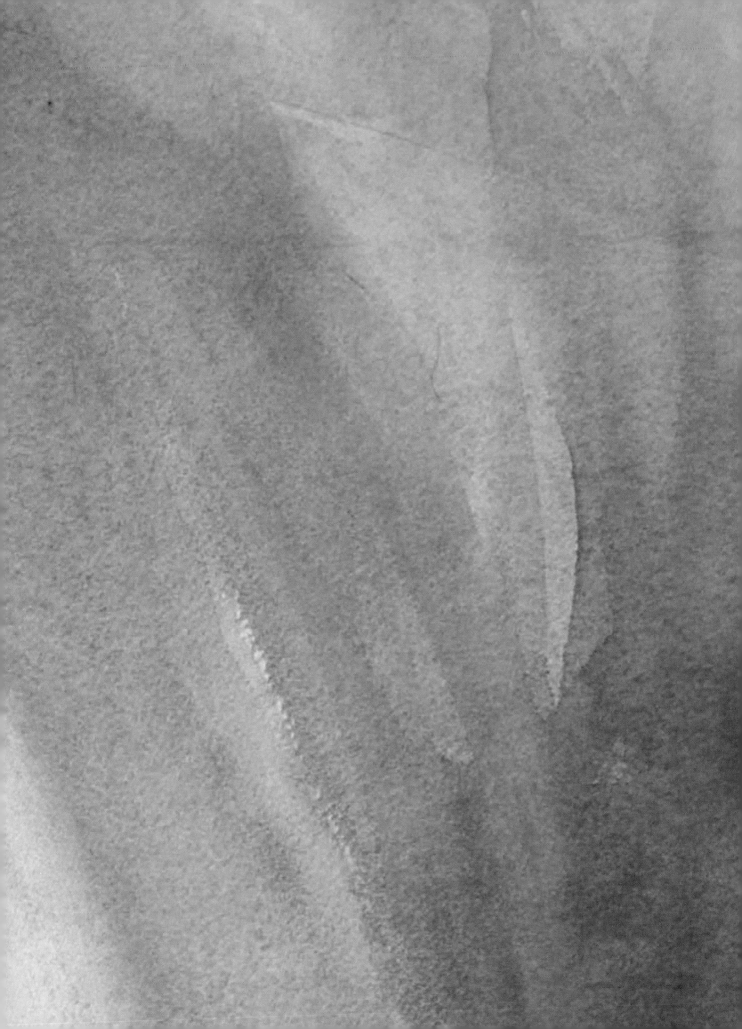

II

THE GREAT SACRIFICE

For God so greatly loved and dearly prized the world that He even gave up His only begotten Son, so whoever believes in (trusts, clings to, relies on) Him shall not perish, but have eternal life.

JOHN 3:16

The Shadow of the Cross

Holy Child, sweet Lamb of God,

for Whom the world could find no room,

You lived in the shadow of the cross

from manger bed to empty tomb.

And even as God spoke The Word

that framed the universe in space,

He saw You nailed upon the cross

as You lay dying in my place.

Great God of mercy, God of love,

May I embrace Your sacrifice,

and live in the shadow of the cross,

no longer I, but Christ!

Infinite Love

Infinite Love displayed for me
the day of my Lord's Calvary.
Did sin demand so great a price?
Indeed! God's utmost sacrifice!
In that great hour, Love lay down
His Life, that, in Him, I be found.
O, sing to me, Song bittersweet.
Rejoice, my soul, rejoice and weep!

Beloved

As I behold
Your wondrous cross
I seek to understand
the mystery of
that sacred cost
recompensed for man.

I cannot know
all reasons why;
my finite thoughts, too few.
But this one thing
Golgotha cries,
I am beloved of You.

Crown of Thorns

A crown of thorns, how could it be?
Of gold perhaps ~ bright, shimmering.
Or, costly jewels, set with care
would best adorn the Fairest of Fair.
A crown of roses with fragrance sweet,
or, victor's crown of laurel wreath
would better suit my Savior's head.
He wore a crown of thorns instead.

The soldiers knew not what they did,
for, in the thorn, a mystery's hid:
the thorn, God's curse upon the land
resulting from the sin of man.
That sin, Christ bore upon the cross;
a crown of thorns ~ the perfect choice.
He wore my curse at Calvary,
that I might wear His victory.

Upwards to a heavenly home

to stand before a holy God.

What can fit me for the right?

'Tis the blood!

All else encumbers my ascent

All deeds, all thoughts withstood ~

All except that crimson flow.

'Tis the blood!

Fair mystery! A robe of white

Adorns me as a holy shroud.

What price this costly garment pure?

'Tis the blood!

A crown of life with precious jewels

Now placed upon my lifted head.

What stains the hands that place it there?

'Tis the blood!

What can, Eternity, sustain?

What proves the Sovereign love?

A Lamb predestined to be slain.

'Tis the blood!

Jesus, righteous Son of God,

Upon the cross, for me endured.

What yet availeth much for me?

'Tis the blood!

The Offering

Oh, to appease the heart of God.

Holy, so holy is He!

What measure of offering could be made

that satisfied He'd be?

Suppose the myriad stars in heaven

all blinked in one accord ~

t'would be a simple feat for Him.

They too obey His word.

The angels in continuum

sing to His glorious name.

Though sweetness to His listening ears,

insufficient all the same.

Mankind makes its offerings ~

a desperate attempt

to satisfy God's righteousness ~

His judgment to preempt.

But God upon His throne on high,

knowing our vain quest,

with a love unfathomable,

left His place of rest.

Since blood of bulls in sacrifice

could not His pleasure bring,

nor satisfy the toll of sin,

God gave The Offering.

A body He prepared for Christ

Who said, "Thy will be done".

The Offering for sin of man

was God's most precious Son.

The shedding of the blood of Christ ~

eternal mystery!

God's heart was wholly satisfied

that day at Calvary.

Come one, come all to heed the call.

The door is opened wide.

Receive you now God's Offering ~

The love of Jesus Christ.

The Cross of Christ

The cross of Christ,

Who can bear?

It is for Him to own.

Yet, I myself

Am affixed there

In Him and Him alone.

He, my strength...

He, the power

For me to overcome.

In temptation's

Darkest hour,

His cross becomes my home.

I hide myself

Within the veil...

The shadow of His wing

Brings peaceful rest

As I prevail

O'er every evil thing.

From cross to grave

To risen Life...

Our hope, our joy, our All.

Oh, Sovereign Lord,

You own the right,

And at your feet we fall.

Crowned with Glory

A glorious crown doth now adorn
that sacred wounded Head
Who reigns as King, but once was scorned
and given up for dead.
Redemption sought...the debt was paid;
the price...God's only Son.
The sin of man, the whole, was laid
upon the sinless One.
But death, that long opposing foe
had not the means nor power
to hold Christ in its world below
in that final hour.
With justice served, the Son broke forth
Emblazoned from above
with rays of righteousness and truth,
and radiating Love.
Jesus, fair and precious Lamb,
Arisen to Your throne,
You are Lord, the great I Am.
We pray, "Thy kingdom come."

Destined for the Throne

Enamored by these worldly goods ~
Oh, Lamb of God, how can it be
when I am destined for the throne
eternally to rule with Thee?
These trinkets of a fallen world
would fain consume my every thought.
Alas! Thy riches far outshine
the fairest bauble sold and bought.
Lands and houses, gold and such
require my all to pay the price.
Yet, Thou hast purchased by Thy blood
True Life. How great the sacrifice!
Lord, by Thy grace, I now lay down
my life with all its vain pursuit
to live in Thee, the One True Vine,
perchance to bear eternal fruit.

No sacrifice could be too great

to lay before that Sovereign Head

Who lay upon a wooden cross

bruised for my sin, in my stead.

Jesus, may I here be found

faithful to Thy gracious call.

As Bride-elect, I fain await

Thy beckon when this earth will fall

away from me, as Spirit wings

bear me up in loving arms

across the threshold to my Love,

secure, eternally, from harm.

Master, Lord, humbled am I

to sit with Thee upon Thy throne

to ever glorify Thy name

for Thou art worthy ~ Thou, alone..

Sing a New Song

Sing a new song, redeemed of the Lord.
Come boldly to God's throne of grace
With lifted head and countenance bright,
Salvation's joy upon your face.

Sing of Christ's atoning work...
His cross e'er bids us enter in,
Our conscience sprinkled by His blood,
Made pure, no shame, no quilt of sin.

Behold the risen Lamb of God,
Our punishment, His body bore.
He...our Champion, Victor, King...
Who intercedes forevermore.

Jesus, Son of God's great love,
We hail Your High and Holy Name,
And sing with fervor Love's new song.
Outrageous mercy, ours to claim!

Passion

Impassioned Lord of Truth and Grace,
You trod this trail of human woe.
With humbleness, You left Your place
of glory, joining men below.
With bold authority, You spoke
the Truth of God to all who'd hear.
With meekness, You endured the strokes
that broke the curse of sin and fear.
You hung between two common men,
identifying with our shame.
And by Your death, we enter in
to Life found only in Your name.
Great fount of love within You found
poured forth the day You bled and died.
No greater passion held You bound
than for Your Father, glorified.
Faithful Son, whom God did send,
redeeming man from death's great pall,
sweet Lamb slain solely for our sin...
now, King of Glory, Lord of all.
Lord, breathe your risen Life in me.
Impassion me to glorify Thee.

 The Gift of God

Behold, what manner of love is this
That God would give His Only Son
As sacrifice for fallen man
That His own child we could become.
A love so vast, so full of grace,
A love the world had never known,
Made manifest to us the day
That Jesus left His heavenly throne.
Oh, Love-descended to the earth...
This frame of dust, Your humble abode...
Resting sweet in Mary's arms ~
But, soon, Your time to bear our load.
The glory of the cross of Christ...
Great pinnacle of Love expressed...
God's provision for our need...
The gift of His eternal rest.
Oh, Love-ascended to Your throne...
Your risen body glorious...
Adorned in righteousness and truth,
We, too, shall rise victorious!

III

YIELDING

Believe in and on the Lord Jesus Christ...that is, give yourself up to Him, take yourself out of your own keeping and entrust yourself into His keeping, and you will be saved.

ACTS 16:31

Surrender

Lord, I give myself to You.

Do with me what You want to do.

Be it great, be it small,

Be it nothing at all,

I give myself to you.

I will not be fearful, but trust.

I will not be hasty, but wait.

Lord, show me Your will

While I 'm waiting here, still.

And make the pathway straight.

You want, not my hands, but my heart,

And first, not my voice, but my ear.

Lord, open my eyes,

Lift the veil, grant that I

Might respond to what You make clear.

Lord, I give myself to You.

Do with me what You want to do.

For Such a Time as This

For such a time as this,

Thou bringest me

from life of emptiness

to learn of Thee:

to fill my heart

Thy grace impart

to turn my soul's remiss;

Thy servant be.

For such an age as now

Thou dost prepare

my mind for knowing how

to stay aware:

to know Your voice

to seal my choice

as I, Your truth allow

its freedom there.

Lord, Thou dost hold all time

within Thy hand.

Eternities all chime

Thy sovereign span:

but grant Thy power

this very hour

that I might share in Thy

predestined plan.

Clinging

Lord,

May I find my all in You ~

no more clinging to possess

what this world affords anew.

Only in You, I am blessed.

You alone ~ my heart's desire.

All else pales before Your face.

Radiant One, send Your fire,

consuming all that takes Your place.

Holy Spirit,...brandish...sever.

Tenderly, Your grace impart.

Break me, bind me, find me ever

clinging to that One True Heart.

Child of Grace

Could I but write fair sonnets, Lord,

to tell of Your great love,

I would pen the cleverest words

that evermore were heard.

Could I but sing melodious tune

to praise Your wondrous name,

then all of Your creation would

join me in my refrain.

Could I but speak Your lofty truths

to all who'd lend an ear,

I'd tell of Your omnipotent worth

with proclamation clear.

Could I but paint a portrait, Lord,

of Your redeeming grace,

then all the world would worship as they

gazed upon Your face.

Child, I require no lofty thoughts.

I just want to talk with you.

Clever sonnets, I never sought.

A joyful heart will do.

No artist brush can recreate

My palette of natural hue.

Now gaze upon My hills, My sky.

I painted them for you.

Fret not what you can do for Me,

but, this I long to do ~

to lavish you with tenderness,

with My love ever true.

This one thing, you can but bring,

I prize as greatest worth ~

your heart, your life surrendering

will find in death, its birth.

Into your sweet life, I will weave

My verse, My thought, My art.

I will sing My song through you.

Yield unto Me, your heart.

When I see you face to face,

rejoicing, I will cry,

"Come unto to Me, dear Child of Grace,

My finest poetry."

 Friend of God

You call me friend,

and friend I long to be.

You wrote Your love

in blood at Calvary.

Your death for me

proved life eternally.

Oh, Lamb of God,

dear Friend, I honor Thee.

Forever now

You stand before God's throne,

pleading for

the ones You call Your own.

Oh, wondrous thought,

I stand among that throng

Whom You call friend.

Yes, to You, I belong.

To be Your friend,

most true, to stand beside ~

uphold Your name

when others scoff and chide.

By grace alone

my loyalty abides.

To You, my Friend,

my God, I am allied.

Highway of Holiness

A Highway of Holiness opens to me.
Released from my bondage, I find I am free
to enter with gladness, its narrow gate,
to travel in freedom this pathway strait.
Redeemed, washed and holy, a saint of the Lord,
I listen, I follow, obeying His Word.
Sweet joy everlasting now rests on my head.
My deserts, once dry, flow with rivers instead.
Encouraged and strengthened, I do not fear
for God, my Redeemer, is ever near.
Sorrow and sighing have all fled away.
What signals this journey? To love and obey.

How Great My God

How great my God?
I cannot know.
My finite mind
too small to show
the span of His
omnipotence.
I can but bow,
my lips confess,
"Thou art, oh God.
Thou knowest best."
How great my God?
Oh, that I could
reach forth my mind
with thought that would
embrace the height,
the depth of Him.

I must content myself to swim

in shallows giv'n

and not contend.

How great my God?

My all in all.

In grace-filled arms

I gladly fall,

and rest in His

omniscience.

My mind, now still,

no more pretense.

Lord, teach me in

my innocence.

A Better Dream

Lord, You healed a withered hand.

Can You heal my withering heart?

Can my dreams that die in You

birth a better dream by far?

Can You make my joy complete

or will I ever grieve?

Will Your presence be enough...

my sorrow to relieve?

You caused the lame to walk.

Can my weakness know Your strength?

You opened blinded eyes.

Can You cause my heart to see?

You unstopped deafened ears.

Can You teach me how to hear

Your wisdom in Your Word

with understanding clear?

You made the dumb to speak.
Can You speak Your love through me?
My quick and cutting tongue
is for You to tame indeed.
Lord, I bow before Your throne
surrendering all I am...
my hopes, my dreams, my everything
I place within Your hand.
Sustain me with Your presence
and grant that I might live
dependent on Your mercy...
the grace You freely give.
Restore my soul within me.
May faith and trust arise
until You are my all in all
and all is satisfied.

The Word

Lord,

Speak forth a word,

a beautiful word,

one only heard

by me.

Surrender Thy truth ~

Thy power to soothe.

May it take root

in me.

Harness my thought.

In You be it wrought

as wind that is caught

in the sea.

You I must know.

Thyself to me show.

Deep may I go

into Thee.

Thy word is my peace ~

all turmoil to cease.

Myself, I release

unto Thee.

The Cry of the Lamb

The law of love must hold me bound

'til Love Himself in me be found.

Hasten, Spirit, to perfect

this infant heart of Thine elect.

Sonship true, Thine ever goal...

Thy sovereign will with mine to mold.

Jesus, elder, Faithful One,

Whose heart reveals the perfect Son,

strengthen, yea, empower me

to die to live...my spirit free

to echo the ancient cry of the Lamb,

"Abba! Father! Yours, I am!"

Finding Life

I know that there will come a time
when I will span that great divide...
the severance of my grieving soul
from all the things I strongly hold...
the things I grasp for my content
that, losing, makes my heart to rend.
But, one fine day I shall awake
and find all joy in Christ who takes
the losing of my life for Him
and grants me grace to enter in
to Life, most real, divine and free.
I in Christ. He in me

A Prayer for Guidance

Father,

Light my way while on this earth I tread.

Only You see through eternal eyes.

Grant that I might, from deceit, be spared

as, trusting in Your Word, I now abide.

Grow me in Your love and in Your grace

that I might love myself and others, too.

Cause Your light to shine upon my face.

May I reflect Your beauty through and through.

Reveal the person I was meant to be

as I rise to meet my destiny.

In the beautiful name of Christ,

Who is my Light,

Amen

My Desire

Oh, to feel the hand of God
reach out to all around
with the gentle, loving touch
that in Him I have found.
Oh, to see each searching soul
through His omniscient eyes;
to have ears so divinely tuned
to hear their heartfelt cries.
Oh, to have obeying feet
so willingly to trod
the paths divinely lighted
by the footsteps of my God.
Oh, to trail the fragrance
of the presence of the Lord;
to speak morsels of wisdom
tasted only in His Word.
Oh, to bring such joy and hope
to every down trod soul:
and witness God's redeeming love
as sinners are made whole.

This is my desire, Lord,

to yield in all I do,

that others might Your glory see

and be drawn close to You.

.....

I hear your humble prayer, my child,

spoken from your heart.

It's My desire to reach through you,

My mercies to impart.

Stay ever close beside Me,

to listen and obey.

I'll speak and always lead you

in what to do and say.

Remember that, I am the Vine;

and you, the branch alone.

Unless My own Life flows through you,

My presence is unknown.

Remain in Me, and I, in you,

will bring My will to pass;

that you might bear eternal fruit –

the only fruit that lasts.

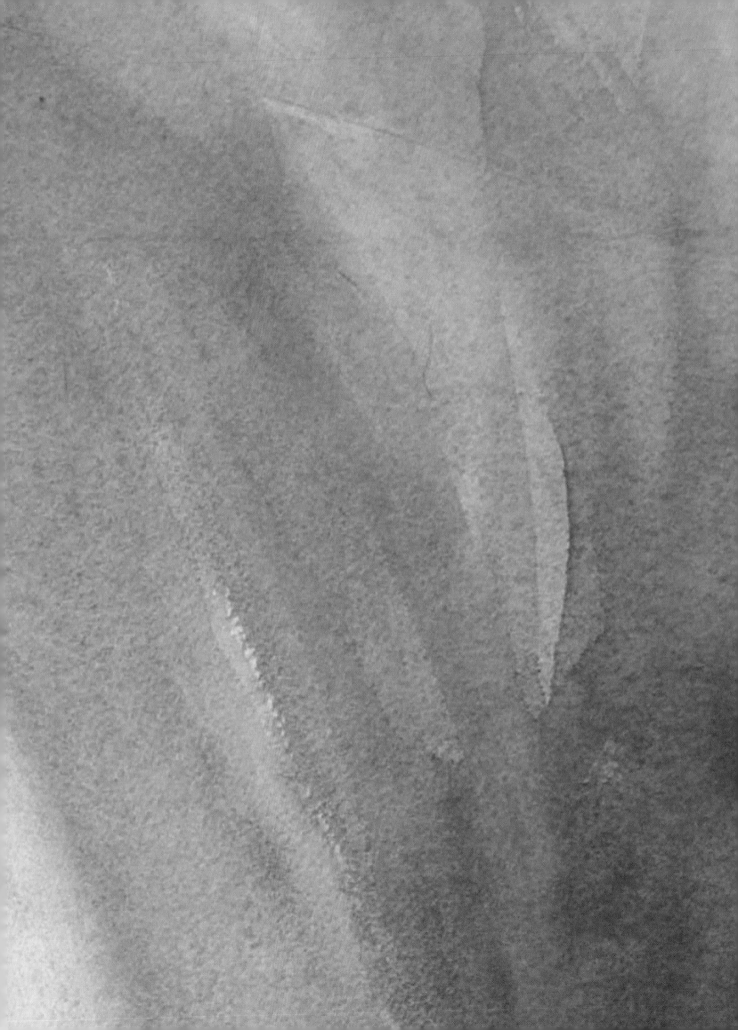

IV

THE LOVE OF GOD

But God, so rich is He in His mercy! Because

of and in order to satisfy the great and

wonderful and intense love with which He

loved us...

even when we were dead in sin, He made us

alive together in union with Christ...He gave

us the very life of Christ Himself...for it is by

grace – by His favor and mercy which you

did not deserve – that you are saved.

EPHESIANS 2:4,5

How high

oh, Lord,

doth Your

love reach?

Enough

to bring

heaven

down to

…you…

How wide, how long Your unfailing love?

Enough to embrace all, for eternity.

How deep

oh, Lord,

doth Your

love reach?

Enough

to lay

down My

life for

you, then

rising,

raise you

up to sit

with Me

..forever..

Love, Enough

Love, enough, to come to me
as I lay dying in my sin ~
to raise my eyes to look on Thee
and cause my heart to understand.
Love, enough, to conquer death ~
Thou, Son of Man, endured the cross
and spanned the length, the height, the breadth
to seek and save that which was lost.
Love, enough, to share Your heart
with all who hearken and believe.
Your Holy Spirit, You impart.
We, gratefully, Your love receive.
Give praise to God, Who loved us first
with love, amazing...
love, enough.

No Greater Love

No greater love hath man than this:
that for a friend, he would lay down,
in sacrifice, his very life.
At once, both heaven and earth resound
with echoes of God's breathed applause,
and joyous stirrings of angels' wings;
while devils, in defeat, take pause,
and men, in reverent voices, sing.
For God so loved the world, He gave
all that He had, His only Son,
who sacrificed His Life to save
those who believe. Oh! Righteous One!
Oh, Perfect Love, thou destined ever
to willingly lay down your life.
Arisen, Thou and we together
eternally. How great the price!

Perfect Love

Perfect love cannot more perfect be.

It cannot grow more dear, nor taste more sweet.

It sings in clearest chords of harmony;

one single note, and foes meet their defeat.

Perfect love, oh, sing your song to me!

Perfect love doth all fear cast aside.

It is not born of arrogance or pride.

It is the lap where kindness doth reside;

and, endless joy and patience both abide.

Perfect love, oh, cradle me inside!

Perfect love, the widest sea can span;

or hold a tiny sparrow in its hand.

It makes not to distinguish man to man;

but, freely gives to all, and gives again.

Oh, love, please cause my heart to understand!

Perfect love cannot an evil know -
will not perform for vanity or show.
It must be e'er allowed to ebb and flow
upon its tide of ecstasy or woe.
Oh, love, just carry me as on you go!
Perfect Love comes down from heaven's throne.
He is the Grace and Truth of God alone.
He seeks my heart to capture for His own.
He is the Christ, God's Lamb, His only Son.
Oh, Perfect Love, to me, enjoined as one!

Love Unconditional

I know that my Redeemer lives.
Each moment of the day He gives
to me the hint of His caress.
He speaks, and I am ever blessed
by Words of comfort, joy and strength.
O! The height, the breadth, the length of
Love unconditional.
Purest joy, in Him complete.
My soul doth ever long to meet
Him face to face. For now I must
be satisfied to place my trust
in unseen Glory soon to be
revealed for all mankind to see ~
Love unconditional.
Thou, Jesus, precious Lamb of God,
Your sacrifice on Calv'ry did
extend to every breathing soul.
O, that each would fain take hold
Your offering and just receive.

Is it too hard to believe in
Love unconditional?
The hardest heart cannot contend
with Love. It melts. Now, enter in
the Lord with His refining fire,
filling all. His heart's desireto
see His captive running free;
the only binding force to be
Love unconditional.
Eternity ~ a worthy span
to praise, to seize, to understand
the goodness of our Sovereign,
Who, by His dying, pardoned man's
rebellion. Arisen, He
ever lives to lavish me with
Love unconditional.

The Measure of Love

How do you measure the gift of love?
It's worth is greater than gold,
outshining myriad stars above
and plummeting depths untold.
It cannot be measured by length of days,
nor passions, though ardent they be.
True love may be captured in a single gaze
sealed for eternity.
Love is a garden of joyous delight
tended with gentlest care.
Seeds of commitment sown in its plight
yield strength for each burden to bear.
Sunshine of laughter, showers of tears
contribute to making love grow,
until the blossom of full love appears ~
its fragrance on others bestowed.
Yes, love is a seed that continues to live
in hearts that receive its embrace.
Immeasurable, forever it gives
abundance of mercy and grace.
Love is a gift whose worth is discovered
by willing to pay the price ~
to give oneself for the sake of another.
Pure love is a sacrifice.

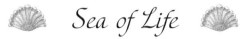 *Sea of Life*

Oh, Sea of Life,
that serves to toss and turn,
on waves, with strife,
each soul cast in your churn.
Dost thou, perchance,
perform your task with malice,
or innocence,
as souls writhe in your chalice?
The latter, thinketh I,
though humble be.
Thou, too, oh, Sea of Life,
know'st Sovereignty.
Your cup, God holds
within His mighty hands.
In strength, He molds,
with wisdom, His great plans.
Each slightest tip
brings billows of despair,
that He might dip,
with tenderness of care,
His sovereign hand endued
with saving grace;
His love, soul's anchor sure,
in storm's embrace.

The Open Secret

What is the secret, slightly hidden
behind that twinkle in thine eye?
It beckons me. Lo, I am bidden
to make inquiry. So I'll try
to lift the veil, thy soul uncover.
Thy mystery, I must discover.
Why the hint of winsome smile ~
thy coy expression, full of life;
joyous procession, all the while,
essence of spring as thou walkest by.
I must take just one peek inside.
Do not, from me, thy secret hide.

...

If my fairest secret's hid,

it is from those who have not known

my Beloved's plea, His bid,

e're to His Bride-to-be, "Lo, come."

I feel His love, His warming grace,

secure within His fond embrace.

The twinkle in mine eye ~ the spark

of my Redeemer's kindled fire

within His breast, unto my heart;

my smile ~ response to His desire.

My secret, I hold passionately.

Yet, asked, I fain hold forth to thee.

...

Oh! Now it is made clear to me.

Thou art in love; and He, with thee.

Love's Song

Such fullness of joy,
Your sweet presence brings.
Abiding with You,
my spirit, now sings.
Your Word leaves the taste
Of You on my lips.
I dare not make haste,
I savor the kiss.
Your arms comfort me;
with strength, they assure,
together, that we
will always endure.
You draw me so near,
so close to Your breast;
my ears faintly hear
Your lover's bequest.
With You, I remain;
where else can I go?

For love, e'er You came.
Your love, I must know.
Your love, I receive,
and hold in my heart.
I shall never leave.
How could I depart?
Could I swim the sea?
Climb mountains above?
In hell, even be
to withstand Your love?
For me, You requite;
I cannot know how.
I gladly would wipe
the sweat from Your brow.
Forever I sought
this love I have found.
Now fullness is wrought,
to You, I am bound.

Together, as one,
we scale the new heights.
In freedom, I come
to share Your delights.
In love's purity,
my gown, I adorn.
Forever, we'll be
refreshed as the morn.
Oh, Spirit's delight,
this love to embrace.
I, never so bright,
as beholding Your face.
...
Lo, I come to you,
oh, fairest of fair,
to ever renew,
forever to care.
Forever to shield

your heart from alarm.
Now safe, you may yield
and rest in My arms.
Your beauty is more
than rubies and pearls.
Your charm, I adore;
around Me, it swirls.
For you, Bride, I died
a sinister death.
In Me, now abide
My love, oh, My breath.
Forever, I cling;
forever, I hold
your love offering,
your body, your soul.

The Dance

I danced before my Lord today;

around, around Him I did twirl.

His eyes of love, to me, did say,

"I joy in you, my little girl;

you are to Me a pure delight ~

arise, my child, on wings take flight."

Such freedom, I have never known.

I wept before His love expressed;

and danced, and danced around His throne,

in innocence, nothing repressed,

while joy remained upon His face

His love to me, my fears erased.

I gathered up His kingly robe;

its purity, I did adorn;

and lightly on my flesh it rode;

within its freedom, I was born.

I danced for my Lord's eyes alone.

His gaze to me did never roam.

Suddenly, I was His bride;

now twirling in my gown of white.

Such beauty I did feel inside,

as on and on into the night,

His gaze did e'er remain on me.

I knew what love was meant to be.

I know not where my Lord will lead;

this only, that I'll follow there.

My captive soul will ever need

to feel His eyes of loving care.

Enjoined to Him, my soul entranced ~

together live, together dance.

Forever live, forever dance.

Oh come, dear saints, unto your Lord.

Arise, arise to take your place.

Together, move in one accord,

beholding Christ, as face to face.

We'll dance Love's Song in harmony,

His glorious bride forever be.

Pure Love

Pure love of God, You hold me bound

when less than love in me be found.

As, deep inside, my sin I see,

I rest beneath Love's canopy.

And as I fail To do Thy will,

Love whispers to My heart, "Be still

and know this God whom sin doth wound.

Grace flows freely from His throne."

Oh, undeserving child am I

that Christ, for all my sin, should die.

Fair Son of God enthroned above,

Who ever bears the wounds of Love,

how can I fail to honor Thee

with all the days Thou givest me?

V

BLESSED BE THY NAME

Praise the Lord! Hallelujah! Praise O servants

of the Lord, praise the name of the Lord!

Blessed be the name of the Lord from this

time forth and forever!

PSALM 113:1-2

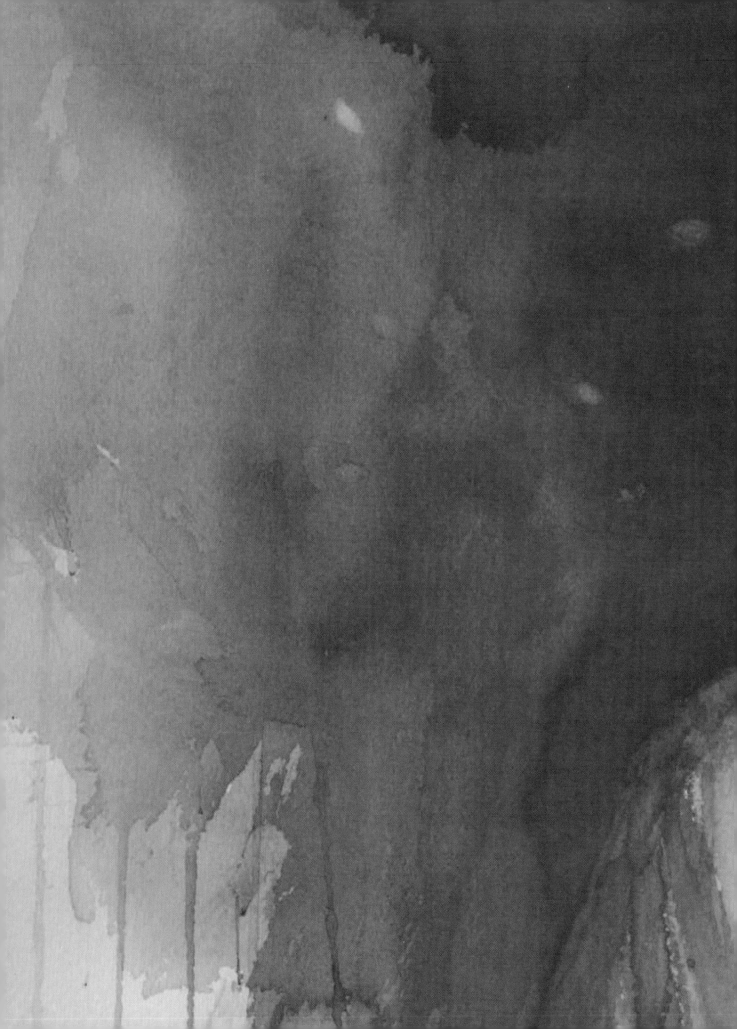

Bread of Life
(True Communion)

Evermore, I'll feed upon the Bread of Life ~

my sustenance for all eternity.

Nevermore, dependant on this earthly life ~

it profits not, nor feeds the core of me.

Livings Words delivered from my Savior's lips,

nourish the aching, longing of my soul.

One life~sustaining morsel from His fingertips,

applies He to my heart. I am made whole.

Daily, will I sit at my Redeemer's feet.

Lo, He beckons always, "Come and dine.

Partake ye of My body, My communion sweet".

He whispers, "I am thine and thou art Mine."

The fragrance of His body, broken, fills this place ~

sweet savour to appease the heart of God ~

That I might come before Him, all my sin erased,

drinking from the fountain of His blood.

Glory, honor, praises to the precious Lamb.

Eternal Life within His power to give.

Dear Son of God, True Manna of the Great I Am.

Only by Your presence, can I live.

The Way, The Truth, The Life

So many voices, what do they say?

"Follow me, I know the way."

But, One Voice says,

"I Am the Way."

One proclaims, "I know the truth.

Hear my sayings, wise and sooth."

But, One Voice says,

"I Am the Truth."

Today's voice says, "Believe in self,

and you will have fulfilling life."

But, One Voice says,

"I Am the Life."

Rose of Sharon

A garden retreat,
where myriad fragrant blossoms
doth unfold.
Yet, none so sweet
as blooms the Rose of Sharon
in a soul.

Jesus, Our Only Hope

Jesus, fair and righteous One ~
our only hope of paradise found ~
Word of God, borne of the Son,
to all who fall within the sound.
Hear, oh hear, His plea to come ~
to taste the sweet and precious fruit
from branches of the Tree of Life.
Relinquish every vain pursuit.
Eternity sits at the door
of every heart, each breathing soul.
Two worlds lay waiting to explore ~
lakes of fire or streets of gold.
Believe the Word, the risen Lamb ~
Eternal One, Faithful and True.
The Lord, your God, the great I AM
has come to earth to rescue you!

Light

Behold the many faceted Christ
in Whom no shadow of turning lies ~
Holy prism illumining earth
reflected in man in whom Thou'rt birthed.
Myriad reflections compose the sea
of God's redeemed humanity.
Here a glimmer, there a spark,
each catching the essence of a Son~kissed heart.
Rainbow of colors, distinctive in hue ~
a celebration of wonder, this crystalline milieu.
One body, ingathered, all unto the Flame
Who bathes all in glory who honor His name.
Living and dancing in glorious Light,
beholding the face of her Lord, shining bright.
Betrothed, now preparing herself for the day
her bridegroom will come and sweep her away.
Eternal glory awaiting the Bride,
forever rejoicing in Love's paradise.

Living Water

My well seems deep with vast supply

until my Savior passes by.

You ask me softly for a drink.

I, then ponder and rethink...

to draw upon my limited source

will not suffice. And with remorse,

I must confess I do not have

what I nor others need to live.

Your small request serves only to

reveal my lack... my need of You.

My well is shallow. Lord, You must

supply me from Your ample trust.

Oh, Living Water, welling up

within this frail and lifted cup,

now quenching me ~ an endless course

of sovereign love from Christ, my source.

Wellspring of Life, dear fount in me,

flow all sufficient for the need.

Fount of Life

Break forth, oh joy of Water Living!

Cascade in torrents o'er my soul.

Dear Fount of Christ, forever giving

abundant Life to make me whole.

You lead me by Thy waters still...

calm pool of peace and harmony,

And bathe me with Thy love until

I rest in Thy security.

River of Life, you carry me

to places led by Thy strong hand.

May I, by faith, Thy glory see

when nought my mind doth understand.

Refresh me, fill me, overflow

my life with Thine own Spirit pure.

And cause me evermore to know

Thy passion that I might endure.

King of Liberty

"Liberty!" Take up the cry,

heralding your coming Lord!

In clouds of glory from on high

He comes with His reward.

All creation groans to be

delivered from the fall of man.

Behold! Your King of Liberty

upon His earth shall stand.

Every eye shall look upon

The Lamb of God whom they have slain.

He rides, emblazoned as the sun,

yet, bears the crimson stain.

Kings and priests of His domain,

viceroys sanctioned by the blood,

look up and sing the great refrain,

"Come, Holy Son of God!"

Freedom, fully realized,

as faithful souls behold His face.

With passion burning in His eyes,

their chains, He doth erase.

Yet, multitudes beholding Him

will weep and mourn, their sins bewail.

True judgment from the risen Lamb,

will all their voices, quell.

Come now hearken to His plea.

Refuse your Christ no more.

The time is short. True Liberty

awaits your opened door.

The Door

I Am the Door

to Life from darkest night.

Come now, explore

My mystery, My delight.

Riches untold

await, as in you go.

Your future holds

more promise than you know.

Just step within...

surrender to My strength.

Exchange begins...

My power for the weak.

Though every trial

might seem your enemy,

your self denial

will lead you into Me.

I, only I,

can cleanse your sin sick heart.

Bring now, your life...

My Life I will impart.

Divine exchange...
the Life you long to live.
All that remains...
for you to freely give
your power weak.
Just place it in My hand.
Then mercy speaks,
"Dear child, come. Enter in."
Why did I grieve,
relinquishing my power,
when such relief
awaited me as showers
of God's great joy,
cascading, filled my soul.
Dear Christ, The Door,
Your strength has made me whole.

# Eternal God

Thou, oh God, Who art eternal,

having no beginning and no end,

hath condescended to enter into

the timely sphere of Thine own creation,

to take on the mortal flesh of man,

that the Divine Life of the creator

might inhabit the body of the creature ~

...a most perfect union...

Thou, oh Bread of Heaven, received

nourishment from a mother's milk.

Thou, Omnipotent One, received

the protection of a parents' love.

Thou, Omniscient One, increased in wisdom,

listening to the scribes in the temple,

ever inquiring of them.

Thou, Judge over all, received

the circumcision under the Law.

Thou, most Beloved of the Father, increased

in favor with God and man.

Thou, oh Perfect One, submitted to
the baptism of John to fulfill all righteousness.
Thou, oh Son of God, learned obedience
through the things which Thou suffered.
Thou, oh Grace and Truth of God, received
no mercy, while being crucified as a blasphemer.
Thou, oh Righteous One, Who knew no sin,
was made to be sin for all men.
Thou, Immortal One, taking on mortality,
yielded Thyself, even unto death.
Thou, oh Glorious One, endured the shame,
..even of the cross...
that Thou, Perfect Love, might conquer death
and bring many sons to glory.
...Thou art.....
and because Thou art, I am.

King of Glory

Open my eyes, Lord,
that I might behold
Your transcendent glory,
Your wealth, manifold.
Shine forth Your light in
my heart. Boundless grace!
Your glory revealed in
Christ's beautiful face.
Jesus, dear Jesus,
Your brightness dispels
infinite night. By
Your gaze I am held
captive. Sweet bondage!
O merciful chain!
Secure me. Release me
from selfish acclaim.

 # Son of God

Jesus, ever rejoicing One,

Delight of the Father, faithful Son,

Master Creator, living Word,

Eternal Wisdom, Sovereign Lord,

To You, we owe our highest praise.

In gratitude, our cup we raise.

Dear Jesus, from Your bounty fill

our treasures that our lives might yield

a fruit far better than pure gold ~

an increase, rich and manifold.

Gladden our hearts with sunlight pure

as we uphold Your justice sure.

Your presence sent in warming rays

bathes us gently all our days

as we behold with lifted face

Your beauty packaged in Your grace.

Begotten in the bosom of

the Father, sent to us with love,

You show us Him Who is unseen ~

You shine Him forth, affect the means

to bring us close within the Three

that we might ever rejoice with Thee.

The Good Shepherd

(taken from Psalm 23)

I

I Shall Not Want

Jesus, Shepherd of my soul,
my every need, Thou dost behold
with eyes of love through all my days.
I rest in fields beneath Thy gaze.
Still waters, Thou dost lead me by
to quench my thirst and thus provide
sweet restoration for my soul.
I am content, replete, made whole.
Thy life, most gladly You lay down
for me, Your child. May I be found
ever faithful in all I do
unto others as unto You,
grateful for Thy care for me.
All around, Thy grace, I see.

II

Paths of Righteousness

Righteousness, the path You choose
for me to walk to honor You
and glorify Thy holy name.
Lord, may I e'er from sin refrain.
If to temptation I succumb,
then unto Thee I swiftly run
and bow before Thy throne of grace.
Forgiveness rests upon Thy face.
Guilt and shame, both from me flee
as I confess my sin to Thee.
The scars of love etched in Thy hand
cause me to know, to understand
that never, never You'll forsake
this child born of that awful fate.

III

Fear No Evil

Through valleys draped in shadows pall,

as thoughts of fearful prospects all

rush in to seize this heart, Thy home,

I cry to Thee, "I am Thine own!"

Dispel this darkness, Lord of Light.

Sweet Presence, see me through this night.

Thy Word, a lamp to light my way

brings comfort...peace...that I might stay

the course...the path Thou dost prescribe.

Never alone...You, by my side.

Thy vict'ry was complete that day

You rose to Life from death's dread sway.

Thine enemy still stalks around

seeking to destroy, tear down

the faith of this, Thy child of grace.

With anger etched upon Thy face,

You hurl Thy rod to intercede.

Safe and secure, I watch him flee.

Evil presents no fear to me

while trusting Whom I cannot see.

IV

Repast

A table heaped...such grand repast...
prepared by Thine own hands. I scarce
can take it in. Words fail me now.
With thorn imprinted on Thy brow,
You serve me in Your gracious way.
I am undone in Love's great sway.
Though enemies may look upon
this feast of love, I cannot come
to harm while e'er I look to Thee.
Thy bounty is enough for me.

V

The Annointing

Warm oil of joy, of fragrance light,

anoints this child of Your delight,

cascading down these tendrils fair.

I know Your touch...Your breath...Your care.

Gladness fills my very soul.

Spirit, conquer me...take hold

this heart, this mind, this will, this voice.

Cause me ever to rejoice...

to celebrate my risen Lord

here and now and evermore!

Overflow this lifted cup

that others may perchance look up

and praise Your Name Most High above...

then bow, believe, receive Your love.Evil presents no fear to me

while trusting Whom I cannot see.

VI

Goodness and Mercy

Goodness follows hard after me.
From its net I cannot flee.
Tangled in its merciful web,
by Thy power, I am held
captive to Thy sovereign will.
Cease, my striving soul. Be still.
God is working for your good...
He...your Champion, Savior, Lord.
Work Thy goodness into me
that I might leave a legacy
of faith that all might prosper by
and Thou, my Lord, be glorified.
Jesus, may I ever live
forgiving, just as You forgive.

VII

Forever Grace

I'll live in Thy forever grace

beholding Jesus, face to face.

Eternal Life is mine...assured,

for, by Thy blood, it was secured.

And by Thy Spirit, I am sealed

until the day Christ be revealed.

In clouds of glory, You will come

for this, Your child, to bring me home,

forevermore to dwell with Thee

in love, in peace, in harmony.

I wait in hope against that day.

Jesus, come without delay.

Rejoice! Rejoice! Sing praise, my soul!

Thy Shepherd Good, you shall behold!

King of Kings and Lord of Lords

Hallelujah! Christ is risen!

Sing, o souls, your Easter song.

Join angels' loud proclaim in heaven.

Praises all to Him belong.

Jesus, Son of God, now seated,

Enthroned in Thy celestial realm.

"Holy, holy...", thrice repeated.

Eternal glory to the Lamb.

Worthy, Thou art, Lord and Savior.

All dominion, Thine to wield.

Mighty, merciful Creator,

To Thy sovereignty, we yield.

Christ, Who maketh all complete,

Robed in splendorous majesty,

Prostrate, we fall down at Your feet,

Revering, yea, extolling Thee.

The Lord our God Omnipotent reigns.

Faithful and True ~ The Eternal Word.

On robe and thigh, inscribed the name,

"KING OF KINGS AND LORD OF LORDS"!

 *Creator*

Lord Jesus, we worship You as Creator

of this seen and all unseen worlds.

You have provided immeasurable beauty for us to enjoy.

Your sun rises and touches our faces

with warmth... with life...with hope.

Shadows are cast by its glorious light ~

Shadows that reach their sheltering arms

across the forest floor,

creeping over the carpeted lawns.

Sunrays filtering through windows into our very hearts,

reminding us of a God Who is Light,

Who is faithful to rise on our behalf

each day of our earthly life,

with the warmth of His love,

in Whose shadow we find shelter, comfort and delight.

Rain, blessed rain, bathing your world afresh.

Thirsty ground drinking in its merciful droplets ~

Life springing from the depths of the forest floor.

Cooling waters quenching our dry throats,

reminding us of the quenching power of Your Spirit

flowing from Your throne of grace, bathing our souls.

Life giving, Life sustaining Holy Spirit ~

Rivers of liquid love

Refreshing, renewing, growing the new life

springing forth from deep within each believing heart.

Son of God, Holy Spirit, Merciful Father,

we will worship You, our Creator, for all eternity.

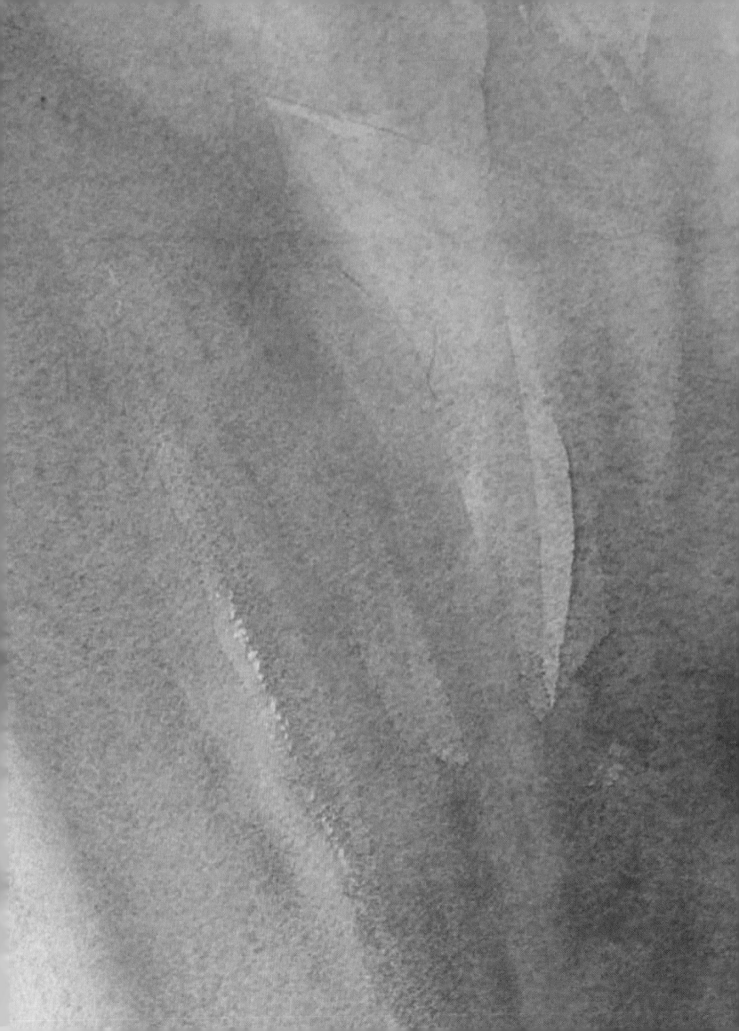

VI

LIFE IN CHRIST

...it is God Who is all the while effectually

at work in you – energizing and creating

in you the power and desire – both to will

and to work for His good pleasure and

satisfaction and delight.

PHILIPPIANS 2:13

The Potter's Wheel

I am my Father's workmanship ~
His plans for me of highest good.
The works prepared afore by Him,
I must embrace, when understood.
He is the potter, I the clay;
upon His sovereign wheel I turn.
In His strong skillful hands I lay,
while grace doth cause my heart to learn.
He ceases not to work in me
His great redemption by the hour,
that I might glorify His name ~
my life infused with His own power.
I rest in His perfecting work;
I strive not to receive His grace;
but, only cause my heart to stay
transfixed upon my Master's face.
Yielded thus, I live in peace,
though perils seek my joy to steal.
Serenity ~ mine to embrace ~
while spinning on my Father's wheel.

Glory

To glorify God is my desire...
to catch a spark from His great fire...
and burn and burn for Jesus' name...
till others catch the joyous flame.
Like incense wafting to the sky,
our prayers arise to Him on high,
Who gathers each within His breast ~
a heart of passion, His bequest.
Oh, dance this dance of fire with me.
Set all the world aflame, and free
dark captives of the evil one.
Oh Spirit, may they see the Son!
Glory...glory...glorious Lord.
Matchless One, by us adored!

Vessel of Mercy

No more striving to attain
a glory tarnished by my sin.
Only yielding to my Lord
to let His mercy rest within.
Receiving from His loving hand
abundant wealth. Yea, He bestows
a far surpassing glory than
my vain attempts could ever know.
Rest, O soul. Receive His grace.
Your foolish struggles only serve
to grieve His heart Who longs to give
what you desire yet don't deserve.
You have nothing more to prove
e'er God has favored you with love.

To My Savior

To look into Your eyes
and know You see the depth of me
yet love me in entirety.

This is paradise.
'Tis beauty that I seek ~
beyond the hills and mountain streams,
beyond fulfillment of my dreams ~
a beauty, strong yet meek.

Held within Your gaze...
through Your eyes, a window wide
unto Heaven opens. Once inside
this sinner stands amazed.

Somewhere Tonight

Somewhere tonight, a tear is dried,

a child feels loved deep down inside,

a man receives the strength to stand,

a neighbor lends a helping hand,

a word is spoken ~ courage lent,

a sinner bows down to repent,

a marriage mends its sacred vow,

a single mom finds hope, somehow,

a friend is there to come along,

a grieving soul receives a song,

a child returns, no more to roam,

a parent welcomes this one home,

a young girl reaches for a star,

a teen is loved for who they are,

a family torn, restores its ties,

a truth is told instead of lies,

a pastor struggles to believe ~

finds grace sufficient for his needs,

a couple in their golden years

receives the faith to calm their fears,

a desperate heart discovers Love...

all perfect gifts from God above.

Somewhere tonight, a prayer is heard...

a presence felt...it is the Lord.

The Color of Love

Jesus, Creator, Lord of All,
Loving and Just in all You do,
You color Your vast, fair handiwork
From Your palette of heavenly hue.
You stepped into Your fallen world,
Shone radiantly with Truth and Grace.
And, willingly, You bore Your cross...
The color of Love on Your face.
On that sacred Easter morn,
You rose in glorious beauty bright.
With one bold stroke of crimson Love,
All sin was banished to the night.
Fair Jesus, risen to Your throne,
Your brush now dipped at Calvary.
By Your grace, I am reborn...
Your Spirit sent to color me.

Color me holy
Bathed in forgiveness by Your grace.
Color me grateful
Upon the cross, You took my place.
Color me joyful
Filled with the promise of the Son.
Color me faithful
That I might hear You say, "Well done."

128

Color me patient

May darkest trials ne'er overtake.

Color me kind

To do unto others for Your sake.

Color me humble

To know my strength is found in You.

Color me loving

Reflecting You in all I do.

Color me fruitful

Abiding in Your perfect will.

Color me peaceful

Resting by Your waters still.

Color me hopeful

Confident of an Eternity...

Ablaze with all the glory of Thee.

Without Your Spirit working in me,

'Tis only for myself I'd live.

So, desperately, I cling to Thee...

Ever dependant on what You give.

Lord, when my life on earth is done

And my frail image fades from view,

May Your beauty rise in my setting sun

And all that remains is the color of You.

God must shatter the image we hold of ourselves in order for us to see Him more clearly. He then shines forth out from the shards of our shattered selves.

 ## The Image

O, shattered image of my self,

you stare at me from deep within.

I cannot bear to look upon

your glory blackened by my sin.

The mask is off. I wore it proud

through all the years of my assent.

But now the naked truth is known,

I can but bow down and repent.

A glorious image now appears

released out from these shards of grace.

A beauty I have never known

seeks now to take my beauty's place.

With grateful heart, I lay me down

and acquiesce to Love's desire

to have His perfect way with me

consuming all with His great fire.

Oh, pure and perfect Love of God

shine forth from deep within my heart

that I might live reflecting You...

no longer I, but You impart.

Reign in Me

Reign in me, oh Lord,
Come, reign in me.
Rule within my heart
That all may see
A life filled with Your love...
Your joy and peace.
Reign in me, oh Lord.
And set me free.
Come now, Spirit, come.
I welcome You.
Do your holy work
And cleanse me through.
Open up my eyes...
Reveal to me
The beauty of my Lord...
His majesty.
Holy Son of God,
You, I adore.
Reflect Your life in me
Forevermore.

Is This the Day?

Is this the day
when life will start anew?
Will joy fain beckon
fresh as morning dew?
Or, will I reckon,
"What am I to do?"
Is this the day
I'll see all my tomorrows?
Will they be brightly
dressed in mornings borrowed,
or promise nightly
elegy of sorrows?
Is this the day
I'll ponder yesteryear;
and see my way
to make my future clear,
or breathe dismay
and end it with a tear?
This is the day
that God has given me.
I know not what
His sovereign plan will be;
but only that
the good remains to see.

Rise Up

Rise up, my soul, rise up with lifted face.

Kiss the Son...bright shining, pure and holy.

Serve the Risen One all of your days.

He is the Lord your God, the King of Glory.

Blessed, so blessed to put your trust in Him

Who holds eternity within His hand.

Run, my soul, seek refuge safe within

the God of Love who gives you grace to stand.

Rise up, rise up and glorify.

Christ the Lord is passing by.

The Trial

We walked our journey, hand in hand,

heart to heart entwined,

enjoined in love to God above,

our wills to His resigned.

On our pathway, we did find

small trials of our faith.

We were courageous and so strong,

fear could not find its chafe.

Then one day, the sun stood still,

the moon refused to glow.

All our understanding, lost.

God's way, too high to know.

Clinging to our thread of faith,

clinging to each other,

we dared not voice our secret thoughts,

for fear, our lack discover.

We held tenaciously unto

the truth that 'God is good'.

And, in our heart of hearts, we knew

He could. Oh! That He would!

A sparrow falls down to the ground,

and not without His care.

Aren't we more precious in His eyes?

Our souls found solace there.

......

The trial has passed, the wind is calm.
The sun has found its place.
Our hearts, now peaceful from alarm,
beat with a steady pace.
Our faith, though tested with the fire,
came forth as purer gold.
Now on our Lord, we more depend.
In love, He doth enfold.
Would we could have stood the test
without the question, "Why?"
Yet, Jesus, in His darkest hour,
uttered the same cry.
Our consecrated walk of faith
may not the trial assuage;
but, patience, with its perfect work,
doth hope to heart engage.
And then, the tenderest love of God
found only in the flame,
doth bind our hearts in one accord,
made sure in Jesus' name.

Patience

How long, oh Lord ?
I stand here strong,
with all my shining armor on.
I know that e'er I see the dawn,
I'll sing the sweetest victor's song
o'er answers from Your heavenly throne.
How long ?

How long, oh Lord ?
The dawn is past;
but in my faith, I still stand fast.
I know no trial's bound to last
beyond my ability to cast
my cares upward that heavenly mast.
How long ?

How long, oh Lord ?
Another day.
There must be obstacles in Your way.
I now must find the words to say
so that Your enemies might lay
down at Your feet, and there to stay.
How long ?

How long, oh Lord ?
O, can it be ?
The problem lies right here in me ?
I'll come to You on bended knee,
confess the sins You make me see -
be grateful through eternity.
How long ?

How long, oh Lord ?
I know not how
to ease this sweating of my brow.
I stand before You naked now,
knowing not what You'll allow
as on this journey I must plough.
How long ?

How long, oh child,
must you remain
within this winter of your pain,
before you know that loss is gain ?
So seek Me now and don't complain.
Your humble praise, I'll not disdain.
How long ?

How long, oh Lord ?
Each waking hour
I feel anew Your strengthening power.
Your mercy bathes me as a shower
bathes the tiny crocus flower
as it springs forth ever higher.
How long ?

At last, oh Lord,

my soul's at rest.

I know that in You I am blessed.

I leave to You the length of test,

to answer me as You see best.

I rest now in Your faithfulness.

I rest.

So rest, my child

in love secure.

Trust My guidance, wise and pure.

My arms are strong, My gaze is sure.

A crown of life as you endure.

Be thou assured.

Peace

A troubled heart,
guilt doth not cease,
a sinner's prayer,
oh, sweet release!
Peace

Anxious thoughts,
unyielding fears,
a supplication,
grateful tears.
Peace

A stormy sea,
a howling gale,
an anchor sure
within the veil.
Peace

A brother scorned,

two hearts divide,

forgiveness sought,

all else aside.

Peace

A soul alone,

temptation's hour,

courage taken,

overcoming power.

Peace

A mind renewed,

a heart believing,

a body yielded,

to do Christ's bidding.

Peace

Knowing God

Lord, keep me from being satisfied with theology,
but may I ever seek to know You by experience.

I cannot know Your mercy
Until I know my sin.
I cannot know Your grace
Until I know my pride.
I cannot know Your comfort
Until I mourn.
I cannot know Your Light
Until I walk in darkness.
I cannot know Your strength
Until I know my weakness.
I cannot know Your love
Until I know my hatred.

I cannot know You as my shepherd

Until I stray.

I cannot know You as deliverer

Until I know my bondage.

I cannot know You as my Bread of Life

Until I hunger.

I cannot know Your living water

Until I thirst.

I cannot know You as my all in all

Until I am nothing.

I cannot know You as my Life

Until I die.

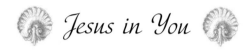 *Jesus in You*

I see Jesus in your eyes:
a peaceful look ~ unhurried,
free from anxious worry;
a serenity from deep within,
no interpersonal battles to win;
a look bestowing honor,
esteeming another;
contented and satisfied ~
I see Jesus in your eyes.

I hear Jesus in your voice:
no boastful song of praise
of your own banner raised;
no ridicule, nor complaining,
all trials remaining;
but, gentle words of reason
said in love and lightly seasoned,
from a heart made to rejoice,
I hear Jesus in your voice.

I feel Jesus in your touch:
a light pat, a fond caress,
a gentle hug, filling emptiness;
a strong arm to lean upon;
a hand extended - warmth of the Son;
a firm push onward, confidence given,
whene'er my soul has backward slidden;
my Savior's love conferred as such,
I feel Jesus in your touch.

A look ... a word ... a touch
no impostor can disguise.
Christ's life of love now lived
through another, crucified.Until I stray.
I cannot know You as deliverer
Until I know my bondage.
I cannot know You as my Bread of Life
Until I hunger.
I cannot know Your living water
Until I thirst.
I cannot know You as my all in all
Until I am nothing.
I cannot know You as my Life
Until I die.

In Thee

In Thee, in Thee,
oh, wondrous thought;
that, in Thyself
all grace is wrought!
Within myself,
my flesh is weak;
but, in Thee, Lord,
I am complete!

In Thee, in Thee,
all joy resides.
Oh, blessed Vine,
I will abide.
Thou, to nourish
my soul's content.
Thou, e'er to keep
what I consent.

In Thee, in Thee,

all power rests.

Thou art supreme,

my soul attests.

Thine, to perform,

mine to believe.

Thine, to bestow,

mine to receive.

In Thee, dear Son,

God's love expressed.

Thine offering

of love, most blessed.

Thou, to my heart

doth rapture bring.

To Thee, oh Christ,

my soul doth cling!

Joy

Joy, unspeakable, full of glory.
Joy, in Love's redemptive story.
For joy, the Son endured the cross;
our joy secured by that great cost.
Joy, the song the angels sing,
as each new soul is born again.
Joy, the fellowship of saints,
as love abounds without restraints.
Joy, the presence of the Lord
that earthly wealth cannot afford.
Joy, to do the Father's will;
at any cost, His Word fulfill.
Joy, to find His perfect peace,
when the trials fail to cease.
Joy, to stand before Christ's throne,
dressed in His righteousness alone.
Joy, to hear His words, "Well done.
Enter in, my child, you are home."

Goodness

God is great, God is good ~
a simple phrase, yet, understood,
must lead me to His throne of grace
to humbly seek His holy face.
For goodness rests in God alone;
filthy rags is all I own.
But, oh, the joy to cast aside
these loathsome rags and then reside
within His arms of mercy, blessed,
adorned with His own righteousness.
Then surely goodness follows me
both now and for eternity!

Looking Beyond

Look far beyond your trial,

Look unto Christ instead.

Let the gazing of your soul

rest on that glorious Head.

He shapes all your tomorrows.

All wisdom, He employs.

Even He looked past the cross

and saw eternal joys.

Look farther than the heartbreak,

and farther than defeat.

Hope waits on the horizon

upon God's mercy seat.

Receive our Lord's provision

specific for your need,

For from Him, through Him, unto Him,

all things consist indeed.

Oh, gracious Heavenly Author
and Finisher of our Faith,
be pleased to do a work in us
to fit us for each day.
May we look beyond our duty,
past our selfish pride and fear.
and through the haze of growing faith
See You standing there...
waiting, pleading gently
for us to step aside
that You might live Your life through us
and be thus glorified.
To touch another with Your love,
bring joy upon a face.....
such fruit is born looking beyond
ourselves and to Your grace.

Looking beyond...beyond all else
'till Christ is seen alone.
Heaven comes down...glory abounds
as He makes your heart His home.

Vision

I asked God for a vision ~
something that I could attain ~
as I yielded my life to Him
to be part of His great plan.
I desired that He might use me
in some significant way,
that others might His glory see
and be led to obey.
I prayed and sought Him daily
in the pages of His Word,
expecting revelation,
but, then, something more occurred.
I found that e'er I sought Him,
my heart grew hungry more
to sit there in His presence
just to worship and adore.
My eyes beheld His sacrifice

poured out upon a tree;
undying Love lay down to die,
then rose to embrace me.
Then, as I walked throughout my day,
my heart was more attuned
to needs of those around me;
by their cries, I was consumed.
I began to see God's love expressed
through eyes touched by His grace;
and others did His mercy see
upon my caring face.
Simple, yet significant,
to walk thus in His light.
I asked God for a vision,
and, He gave to me His sight.

Gladness

Gladness fills my heart today ~
anointing oil of God's delight,
warming me with inner fire,
fueling my utmost desire
to keep my Lord before my sight.
Nectar of joy, remain, I pray.

I feel a fluttering within ~
fond skipping to a distant beat ~
drums of passion for my Lord
in tune with His Eternal score.
Within this sacred dance, defeat
must flee, devoid of guilt of sin.

Gladness, sweet, entices me ~
Entrée to joy's Eternity.

Fellowship

Sweet fellowship,
redeemed hearts skip
in joyous harmony.

Christ's love abounds,
there then resounds
the Spirit's symphony.

 The Gentle Call

Rocking at his mother's breast,
the tiny infant thus receives
God's provision for his needs
to nourish his yawning, stretching frame.
But, with much more he's surely blessed ~
her gentle touch, her loving gaze;
enough soul~joy to fill his days.
Tenderly, she speaks his name.

Skipping o'er the rocks of youth,
the manchild reaches toward his goals
to seize the prize his eye beholds,
while reassured by loving hand.
And gentle words both firm and sooth
still guide his wanderings e'er near
within the distance he might hear
his name resounding through the land.

Rocked upon the sea of life,

where only strong hearts can endure,

and comfort is no longer sure,

he must stand tall and be a man.

But, deep within this heart of strife

remains the need through all his days

for gentleness of touch or gaze ~

his name adjured by kin or friend.

Rock of Ages, strong and wise,

from Whom no deepest need is hidden,

Justice~Served and mercy driven,

seeking from His heavenly shoals,

looking through omniscient eyes

that search this sea of wandering souls,

this humble man, He now beholds.

Gently how his name He calls.

Standing on the Solid Rock,

the man now faces life, complete ~

his soul no longer in defeat;

but, mighty through the Savior's power,

when trouble at his door doth knock,

and raging battles, him surround,

he listens for the gentle sound ~

his name, God~breathed, to calm the hour.

Faith:

a tiny seed,
embodied power,
to meet the need
of every hour;

planted in
each searching soul ,
to draw us near,
Christ to behold;

to reach within
the Savior's breast,
so great salvation
to request;

to turn from all
our wickedness,
toward mercy, love,
and righteousness;

to speak to
mountains in our way;
to trust in Jesus
day by day;

to lie down at
the Master's feet
when e'er our souls
have met defeat;

to grace with song
the darkest night,
and overcome
tormenting fright;

to battle all
a lifetime's woes -
the beast within,
and outward foes;

to inherit from
the Trinity,
and partake of
such divinity.

May so great faith
in me be found,
that, to my Lord,

But, should great faith
allude me then ,
may faith sufficient
rise within

to know that, though
I can't reach up,
my Savior bends,
my heart to cup

within His hands
of mercy sure ;
He covers me,
I can endure.

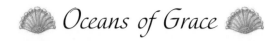 Oceans of Grace

Ocean of grace, wash over me ~
Love poured out beyond compare.
Open my eyes that I might see
the labor of Thy tender care.

Thou, dresser of this wayward soul,
bestowing favor, underserved...
pruning, shaping, making whole,
to the end that Love be served.

By Thy tide, I stand or fall...
all things toward eternal good.
I fain surrender to Thy call,
engulfed by Thy relentless flood.

Grace, conceived by Spirit...water,
borne on waves of sacrifice ~
glory of our God and Father
reflected in the face of Christ...

Manifest Thy love and freedom.
Make me know true soul's delight.
Train my heart in every season
to live within Thy perfect Light.

A Prayer of the Church

Our Heavenly Father, ever the same,
Most hallowed is Thy glorious Name.
Thy kingdom come within our hearts.
Thy will be done...Thy grace impart.
We're thankful for our daily bread.
From Thy Word, we're fully fed.
A thousand mysteries, each word holds.
With lifted veil, Thy truth unfolds.
Forgiven, we stand, in Thy pure Light,
Made sure by Jesus' sacrifice.
May we forgive, as Thee, above,
To image forth Thy perfect love.
Delivered from evil, faithful, we stand
Shielded by Thy strong right hand.
For Thy kingdom, we now live.
Strengthened by Thy Spirit, we give
Honor and praise to our ever King,
Who is for us, our everything.

VII

AMAZING SPIRIT

And I will ask the Father, and He will give

you another Comforter (Counselor, Helper,

Intercessor, Advocate, Strengthener and

Standby) that He may remain with you

Forever...

The Spirit of Truth.

JOHN 14:16;17

Amazing Spirit

Amazing Spirit, God divine,
You shine Your light and I can see
all that Jesus means to me
for all eternity and time.
You move upon this body frail
to form, to mold, to make anew
till Jesus' life comes into view.
Step by step, You lift the veil.
I yield myself unto Your care...
embrace divine conformity
to this great end, that all may see,
not me, but Jesus standing here.
Life companion, loving Friend...
Joyous journey without end!

To the Holy Spirit

Dear True Companion of my soul's journey,
without Your strong assist, where would I be?
Though darkness seeks to make my path obscure,
Your constant glowing Light doth guide me sure.
And, on Your wisdom, I can e'er depend,
when all my reasonings, no answers lend.
You comfort mine affliction through the night,
and, bring Your healing balm, oh, soul's delight!
Your sure correction when I go astray,
doth serve to keep my heart out of harm's way.
Oh, Friend, enabler for the very hour,
when I, by faith, rely on Your great power.
You, Who extend, with might, the hand of God
to all here, who believe, as on we trod.
And, wonder of them all, You speak to me
of divinest Love, too great to be ~
a love poured out for me in sacrifice,
for every sin I own, it doth suffice ~
a love that seeks my soul to fond embrace,
and keep in constant care, 'til face to face,
You carry me upwards to heaven's throne,
present me to my Lord, God's precious Son ~
sweet Lamb of God, then slain for even me ~
that I might be with Him eternally.
Thou, Spirit, guarantee of Sovereign Love,
be all to me my Lord grants from above!

Ride the Wild Horse

Give Me the reins.

I long to take control.

I'll tame your maverick spirit.

I'll free your soul.

You'll find delight

and strength within My will.

We'll scale adventurous heights.

Now dare to yield.

Ride the wild horse

of My Spirit running free.

Cast all your care and follow

the wind and Me.

Free

Holy Spirit, come to me,
come to set my spirit free,
free from what I want to be,
free from others' scrutiny,
free for what You want for me.
Free!

Spirit of God

Spirit of God, descend on me.
Like a dove, alight my heart.
Softly sing Your graceful song.
Tender mercies, You impart.

Quench the longing of my soul ~
in Love's great torrent, baptize me.
Sweet peace of knowing I belong
to God for all eternity.

Show me Jesus. Make Him real ~
to know Him doth all thought transcend.
For love, He did the Father's will.
May I, for love, now honor Him.

Spirit, stay. Encourage me.
I cannot walk the way alone.
Without Your strong empowering,
my weakened heart would frequent roam.

Thou, Gift of God, from heaven's throne,
fair proof of Jesus glorified,
I dare not fail to welcome You.
Oh, trusted Friend, in me, abide.

The Lily

My soul, like a lily, opens to Thee

to drink in Thy goodness,

Thy love and Thy peace.

Rain down from heaven,

Sweet Spirit of God.

Quench now the thirsting

of my lifted heart.

By morning, I savor

the dew from the night.

Evening brings showers

that whisper delight.

Though storm clouds may gather,

they bring me no harm.

I rest in the shelter

of Thy loving arms.

Dress me, my Father,

in glorious array

to mirror Thy beauty

all of my days.

The Lyric of Spring

The winter cold is waning.
Oh, Lord, restore my soul!
May all the chill remaining
be warmed as I behold
the first rewards of springtime,
the sunny daffodils.
The rose begins its arbor climb,
the birds resume their trill.
Through myriad winter seasons
Your faithfulness remains.
You, only, know the reasons,
and, by Your grace, sustain.
Awakened by the lyric,
my soul springs forth to soar.
The warm wind of Your Spirit
breathes life in me once more.

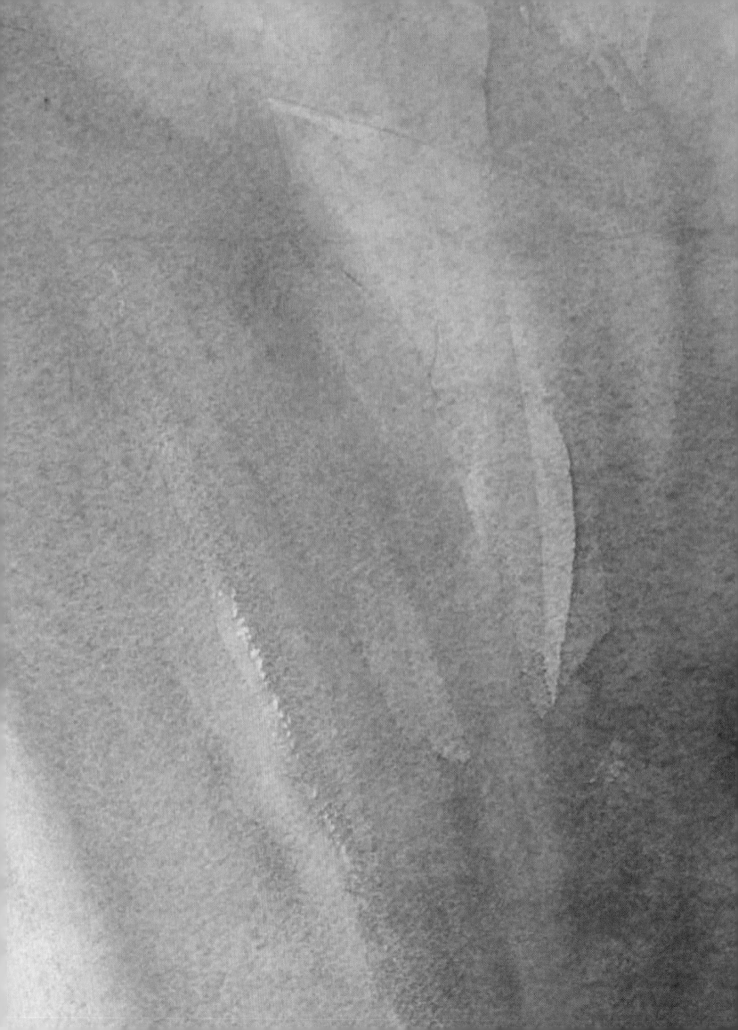

VIII

ENCOURAGEMENT

Wait and hope for and expect the Lord; be brave and of good courage, and let your heart be stout and enduring. Yes, wait and hope for and expect the Lord.

PSALM 27:14

God Knows My Name

I hope in God's unfailing love
though storm tossed waters round me swirl.
No help for me, save from above.
I am my Father's child.

He will not leave me all alone.
The battle is too great for me.
By faith, I come before His throne
and wait expectantly.

With arms outstretched, He welcomes me.
His love for me ~ always the same.
And, on His great palm I can see
He has engraved my name.

No matter what the future brings~
the pain of loss or joy divine~
in this I trust; to this I cling:
I am His and He is mine.

My Father's love will e'er remain.
He hears my cry. He knows my name.

In our suffering, when we run to Christ,
we run straight into the heart of God.

Run Unto Me

Come, and let Me comfort you, My child.
Run to Me and rest in Me awhile.
You do not walk your path of pain alone.
For I, your God, once left My glory throne
to walk the path of suffering and pain
that all My wandering children, I might bring
unto My breast to succor...yea, relieve.
So come and find My comfort as you grieve.
In Christ, I bore your pain upon the cross.
I suffered then for this, your present loss.
Now as you step, by faith, into My Son,
you'll be absorbed in Him and Me as One.
Together, suffering what has been allowed,
you will find strength and mercy, I avow.
In the end, My purpose is not swerved.
And you will know, My child, Love has been served.

Hold Fast

Hold fast, dear saint, to what is good,

though the world around you mock.

Take joy when you are misunderstood;

herein, the war of faith is fought.

Take courage, saint, when faint of heart,

though the battle rages still.

God does to you His grace impart,

as you embrace His perfect will.

Rejoice, dear saint, in grateful praise

in every circumstance of life.

God's eyes of love, with careful gaze,

give constant watch throughout the night.

Be kind, dear saints, to one another,

seeking good, no evil repay.

In Christ, all knit, brother to brother;

diverse, yet set in fine array.

Oh, blessed saint ~ spirit, body, and soul ~

held blameless at that great repast.

God is faithful, Who has called,

to bring you to Himself at last.

Hold fast, dear saint, hold fast.

A Better Song

There is a better song to sing
than lifeless notes, though duty bound ~
A song that seeks my heart to bring
itself enjoining with the sound.
Love, embracing, flowing forth
as Sovereign passion strums the lyre
and tunes my heart to Christ, my source ~
making Him my sole desire.
Lord, course my heart to love You more.
Your love impassions all of life,
and garlands every opened door
with graceful song and glorious light.
Oh, hear the music, faint of heart.
He fills your mind, your body and soul,
infusing each and every part
to captivate and make you whole.

Come, Lord, Come

I trust in You this very day ~
another miracle on its way.
My heart will not shrink back in fear.
Be pleased, Oh Lord. Draw me near
to stand before Your throne of grace
receiving mercy for my faith.
Yours works are done in fertile fields
of faith applied. Its fruit, it yields.
You are able. This I know.
Arise, my Lord, Your works to show.
Reveal Your glory, might and strength
in frames of dust. Cause all to think
upon Your most Beloved Son.
I lift Him high. Come, Lord, come.

Breakthrough

Make way, my King is coming through,
no longer on a burro riding.
A stallion bears His grace and truth
to all who, in Him, are abiding.
All things good and possible
within the presence of the Lord,
Whose Spirit hovers o're the soil
enriched by His oft spoken Word.
Feast your eyes on heaven's glory ~
Jesus, in His majesty.
He is the breakthrough in your story;
the answer to your heartfelt plea.

Breaking through, breaking through ~
no wall too strong to crumble down.
The Lord of glory fights for you.
Believe, receive your breakthrough now!

The Sacrifice of Praise

Father, unto You I offer
sacrifice with trembling hand,
knowing not how this could prosper
Your omniscient plan.

Thread of faith, hold me tightly;
this, my soul, quite wounded be.
Comfort me, Dear Spirit, nightly.
Dark envelops me.

You, I trust. There is no other.
Only You are truly wise.
On this path I may discover
life seen through Your eyes.

But for now, I must retreat.
Lord, shield my heart from all alarm.
Balm of Gilead, such sweet
repose waits in Your arms.

Rose of Sharon, crushed, made whole,
bring fragrance in this desert pain,
until the praise deep in my soul
finds its voice again.

Faithfulness

Faithfulness is precious gold,
proclaiming, "God is in control".
Through circumstances that I hate,
You send Your Word and dissipate
the fear that I am all alone.
Your love secures me to Your throne.
My questions cease, and now I know
You are God. Be pleased to show
Yourself as strong, for I am weak.
While I am still, oh, speak, Lord, speak.
Now unto my uplifted heart,
Your Word of comfort You impart.

"This fiery trial that you endure
will serve to mold My Life in you.
This cross you bear is My means
to bring to pass what now seems
impossible. Yet, glory rests
upon the one who will attest
to My great good and righteousness.
By your faith, I am blessed.
My Only Son endured His cross
and yet despised the shame it brought.
But trusting Me to raise Him up,
He drank that vile and bitter cup.

The means to let my glory through
are painful for they beckon you
to lay your own will down and die
that I might raise you to new life.
The joy I set before you fills
you with great hope, as this, My will,
you now accept above your own.
Surrender sees what I have done."

Oh, Lord, I want to sing this song
and tell the world that all belongs
to You. You are the great I AM.
By your grace, we live and stand
to face a new God~given day.
Oh, Jesus, cause my heart to stay
transfixed upon Your glorious face
that all my doubt might be erased...
that I might glorify Your name.
In all of life, may I proclaim
Your faithfulness to all your own
to see us through...to bring us home.

 The Comforter

I extend my hand to lay it upon

the shoulder of another one

who on its journey is overcome

in sad defeat.

Lord, bring your sweet

consolation in this long hour.

Devastation seeks to devour

this burdened heart ~

this tender flower.

Lord, only You

know what to do.

Listening, my heart just bleeds.

If, for one moment, I could relieve

the pain; but I just sit and grieve.

Lord, You are here.

You love, You care.

These tears of pain ~

The Spirit's release ~

The Father's refrain at Calvary.

My God, You are no foreigner to grief.

You bore it all upon that tree.

Together, we

rest in Thee.

The Gift

I thank You, Lord, I am not strong
enough to weather life alone.
The weaknesses I see in me
force me to come on bended knee,
receiving from Your proffered hand
all I need for life's demand.
No longer, now, will I despise
Your gift to me sent in disguise ~
an offering for me to rest
within Your strength. Oh, weakness blessed!
Each thorn, You send to pierce my heart
that Sharon's Rose might then impart
His fragrance of humility.
From self~reliance, I am free!
I glory in this gift of love.
My lack binds me to You above.
I pray this gift for all the strong
who know not, to You, life belongs ~
who yet are bound by their success.
May weakness pierce their armored breast,
that, yielding, they may seek Your face
and find Your all sufficient grace.

Stand

Dig deep, my child, and touch the omni Source

Whose love and power grant strength to stay the course.

Commit yourself to all you know is true.

My Word, you've sown, bears faith to see you through.

Be not dismayed when arrows pierce your heart.

Come quickly, child, My grace, I will impart.

Stay focused on Your King upon His throne.

Your oft sung praise will make His presence known.

Trust the One Who holds you in His hand.

Embrace his love. Be still. Be faithful.

Stand.

IX

EXHORTATION

Let us exult and triumph in our troubles and rejoice in our sufferings, knowing that pressure and affliction and hardship produce patient and unswerving endurance. And endurance (fortitude) develops maturity of character...that is, approved faith and tried integrity. And character [of this sort] produces [the habit of] joyful and confident hope of eternal salvation.

Such hope never disappoints or deludes or shames us, for God's love has been poured out in our hearts through the Holy Spirit Who has been given to us.

ROMANS 5:3-5

Come Forth

Come forth, oh man of resurrection Life!

Stay not within your grave clothes bound.

Be loosed from bondages of old.

Now grace and truth are in you found.

Put off the old man and his ways.

Put on the new man in the Lord.

Rely not on your arm of flesh.

Come forth at His commanded word.

Reveal the Life of Christ within,

unleashed this day for all to see.

Come forth, come forth, oh, man of God

and set men free!

Waver Not

Waver not, dear saint of God.
Fear and doubt go hand in hand.
Grow up strong in saving faith;
grace will cause your heart to stand.
Praise and glorify your Lord,
fully know that He will keep
all His promises foretold.
He slumbers not, nor does He sleep.
Exult in trials, knowing that
patience is their product best.
From endurance then is born
character to stand the test.
Joyful hope, then manifest,
never serves to bring dismay.
God's great love, His Spirit pours
into your heart this very day.

Significance

Why do you seek significance
in worldly realms so small,
when God, Who made the universe,
now, at your door, doth call?
Why put such worth on praise of men,
whose praises rise and fall,
when you could please the Sovereign,
fair Ruler over all?
Why find delight in earthly goods,
whose beauties fade away,
when heavenly abundance would
be granted you each day?
Why settle for the future hope
of life in heaven spent,
when God extends His pow'r to cope;
your present cares relent.
Yes, Jesus at your threshold stands,
significance to bring,
to mold your life, your dreams, your plans ~
relinquish everything!

Fear Not

Fear not, oh, my soul
of uncertainty;
but, only take hold
of strength given thee.

Be anxious for naught,
but, praise only give.
God's grace is thus wrought.
In hope, thou must live.

Be still, oh, my soul,
and listen for God.
You then will be told
where'er you must trod.

Have faith in your Lord;
You know not His ways.
He's true to His Word
to fulfill your days.

Take rest, my soul, now;
be peaceful and calm.
My Jesus knows how
to soothe with His balm.

Rejoice, spirit, sing!
God's love is assured.
The awe, His cross brings;
for you, He endured.

 Vanity

Vain soul, would thou only on thyself depend,

to still thy passions;

so bent on thy destruction as their end?

Or would thou boldly on thy strength rely,

to mold or fashion

thine own goodness as thine adroit reply?

Thou to thou belie.

Thinkest thou, that thy most clever action

could lure God's fancy;

and stay His hand, or hold His rapt attention?

Or, by thine own repentance thou coulds't purge

thine own vanity;

and thus forever stem that sinful urge?

Thou dost thou indulge.

Soul, could thou by thine intellect discern

all divinest truth;

and cause thyself so willingly to learn?

Or, could thou by thine own appointed reasonthine

own counsel soothpredict,

lo bring to pass, thy future season?

Thou speakest treason.

Behold thy Maker, bow before His throne;

to Him all glory be.

Repent thou soul, lie down before Him prone.

May He then raise thee, His own goodness bring,

to cause thou, soul, to see:

He is the Christ, by Him is everything.

Thou, oh soul, now sing!

True Worship

Praise and worship wear their golden crowns
on heads aplomb, proclaiming the Good News.
With hype and punch, the battle cry resounds.
God's new army sings an upbeat tune.
Redressed in its contemporary style,
The latest high tech systems sound the call.
With bodies swaying, one can't help but smile
and "catch the beat" as the Spirit falls.

Yet, in the frenzied singing, voices raised,
Do we truly worship from our heart?
Or are we just caught up in corporate praise,
and in our Savior's plight we have no part?
Are we full of joy or just aroused?
Does the Spirit burn or are we cold?
Is our ministry of worship housed
in worldly efforts to ignite the soul?
When we sing of Christ upon a cross
with a lively syncopated beat,
Do we truly reverence the cost:
Is our heart then bowing at His feet?
A celebration of His love is sure,
and joy should be the order of each day,
but let us, in our hearts be ever pure
and highly hold the price He had to pay.

Christ moves among us in simplicity,

searching for an entrance for His life

to be reborn in true humility ~

A yielded heart will make the sacrifice.

Hear the Savior, feel His soft heartbeat.

Hear, and then go likewise, do the same.

An apron don to wash another's feet,

A cup of water, offer in His name.

Remove your crowns; lay them all aside.

Expend your life to aid the poor, the lost.

Then Jesus will will indeed rise up inside

And you will know true worship from the cost.

 Success

If success were measured by one's fame,
of scores who could recall one's name,
or all the fortunes one could claim,
then I have failed.

If worth lived in palatial halls,
attended the élitist balls,
or answered only significant calls,
then I have none.

But, suppose the few who knew my name
could always by their lips proclaim,
my integrity did e'er remain;
or on my aid they could depend,
encouragement, I'd ever lend,
and selflessly their needs attend;
or, what if, from my fortune small,
I willingly dispensed to all
who at my humble door did call;
and, if my Maker, I did bless
with grateful praise and faithfulness,
and in His mercy ever rest,
I've met success.

Idleness

Idleness, oh, bitter bread;

at first enticing with its scent

of long and lazy hours spent,

lavishing at heart's content,

when naught is done, though much is said.

But, with each tasty little bite,

one's vision dims until the sight

becomes by day, as if by night,

and sleep beckoneth limbs of lead.

Then all around is laid to waste,

pain and poverty make haste,

fear swells with its acrid taste;

bitterness and wrath are fed,

while languor makes its mocking bed.

Sovereign Freedom

In sovereignty, Thou rulest over land.

All of life within Thy mighty hand.

At Thy command,

a tree doth stand,

or die at root

for lack of fruit,

and seas divide amidst their widest span.

But, what of man? Thou givest freedom's choice.

To mock or praise Thy name, Thou givest voice.

Man seeks his own,

and builds his throne

or bows before

Thee to adore,

while Thou allowest all, in love's rejoice.

Oh, freedom ~ greatest foe or sweetest friend?

Within its throes, my soul doth find its rend.

My heart desires

what God requires;

my flesh then speaks;

resolves made weak;

and, I choose to, instead, my self attend.

The battle ever rages in my quest ~

Love's freedom ever put to fiery test.

Woulds't Thou control

my wayward soul?

'Tis mine to yield;

'tis Thine to wield

Thy power to obey. Oh! Freedom blessed!

 Keep Silent

Keep silent, my lips,
from speaking falsehood;
but, truth only speak,
and, that, when you should.

Keep silent, my lips,
from flattering words,
that seek to impress,
and make me adored.

Keep silent, oh mouth,
from boasting great things,
knowing not what
the near future brings.

Be tamed, oh my tongue,
small rudder of soul;
but, mighty to steer
me out of control.

Be deaf, oh my ears,
to gossiping sound.
May God's love and grace
so much more abound.

Be silent, my heart,
from judgmental thoughts.
May God's purity
now ever be wrought.

Be still, oh my soul;
be swift, ears to hear
the voice of your God;
then, speak His words clear.

 *God's Grace*

How dare I base my prayers on anything
that I may have accomplished by my will.
The thought doth cause my heart to near stand still,
and send upward my spine a deathly chill;
such insult to my Lord this folly brings.

For, what would be the price of God's mercy?
a tenth of all I own, or even more?
to give myself up to some loathsome chore?
to read His Word each day; nay, underscore?
Surely, these deeds would sufficient be.
Or, live my life in such self-discipline -
to eat and drink for nourishment alone,
and, only bare essentials dare to own,
and, spend legions of time before Him prone?
Perhaps my Lord would be moved to give in.

It pains me just to set these words in place,

for, I know that in my heart, in days gone by,

I vainly sought Him thus, I cannot lie.

Repulsive now to me that I did try

to put a price upon my Savior's grace.

Even if I had ten lives to live -

to serve God every minute of each day,

to ne'er let my old nature have its way,

and keep completely out of sin's dread sway,

there would not be enough of me to give

to pay for one sweet morsel from His throne -

one healing touch, my body wounded be,

one moment's peace, my mind's fear to relieve,

one seed of faith, my heart made to believe,

one goodly deed, my will made to achieve,

one whispered breath of life sustaining me.

It is wrought by His grace, and that alone!

 *Judge Me Not*

Judge me not,
you know not where
my life has been
nor do you care,
as, from your perch,
with righteous eyes,
you search for fault
in others' lives.

Judge me not,
you know not where
my Savior leads me,
just take care
that from a heart
devoid of pride,
you, too, within
His will abide.

Judge me not,

encourage me

to hear God's voice,

and then obey.

And I, for you,

will do the same;

together, we

will praise His name.

Judge me not,

just let me be

all that my Lord

desires for me.

Together then,

in harmony,

we'll sing, with joy,

"How sweet to be ...free!"

Crucified

If I proceed to walk in sin
when Jesus' death has set me free,
then all the pain that He endured
avails not me.

Forgive me, Lord, when I refuse
the power of Your holy name.
You, I then crucify anew
and bring You shame.

If I but count all things as loss
to know Christ and His saving grace;
then, His own righteousness adorn
and live by faith...

I, then, have crucified my flesh
that He might live His life through me;
His sacrificial love, He'll pour
for all to see.

All That Remains

This unclean heart lives only for itself.

Possessive love pours forth to all around.

Destruction sits awaiting its dark cue...

Both toward this heart and all within its sound.

Unfailing Love reveals its risen life.

Surrender knows true love beyond compare.

My natural love, once cherished, now lays down.

All that remains is Jesus standing there.

The Love of God in Christ

Why sit around in rash debate
of lesser issues which consume
our thoughts, our energies and sate
our consciences, and yet entomb
the greatest truth in all of life ~
the sacrificial love of God in Christ.

Hours upon hours spent
ravaging each others' minds.
Here a stance, there, consent
until the ebb and flow of time,
while God, perceiving from on high,
with nail scarred hand is beckoning us nigh.

All vain conceit, now lay aside.
With humble heart receive the Lord.
Your intellect puffed up with pride
will only serve to veil His Word
which, hearkened, sets the captive free.
O Lord of Love, enslave and ravish me!

Heart Cry

Lord,

could I but sing Thy song ~

mine own song silent,

least held at bay,

until Thy still small voice might have It's say.

In this my heart doth long

to be compliant.

Could I but do Thy will,

mine own will silent,

least bending

toward Thine omniscient choice, not yet

contending.

To this, my heart doth yield,

though will, defiant.

Lord,

hear You now my heart ~

it's plight, its groaning

to bring You joy

in all its meditations.

Grace, I employ

to do Your generous part,

my part bemoaning.

 Wait on God

Wait on God? Surely you must jest!

Time is of the essence and I need

to work and play at life at such a speed

that at the close of each frenetic day,

I may shut me eyes and gladly say

"I have lived life fully in my quest."

God will have to run to follow me.

I have no time to wait on bended knee.

Wait on God? My hand is at the plow.

Sit you, if you must, at silent prayer.

Perhaps your God will come to meet you there.

But mine is ever urging me to run.

He beckons me, "Be swift and chase the sun."

Waiting is for dreamers. Here and now,

I must about my business be.

I have no time to wait on bended knee.

Wait on God? I never had the time.

But gaze upon the things I have amassed ~

reward aplenty for my ardent tasks.

And yet, I am now too weak to enjoy.

All my strength, this journey did employ.

Were truer riches there for me to find?

Contentment, joy and peace alluded me.

I had no time to wait on bended knee.

.....

Wait on ME. Then follow at My lead.

Be still and listen for My quiet voice.

To walk in step with Me remains your choice.

Time is My design ~ My gift to you.

Eternity rewards what you now do.

Life is meant to be lived at Godspeed.

Kingdom work must evermore be done

In strength gained in the presence of My Son.

.....

Yes, wait on God. Now listen to His plea.

Too late, I saw the value of a life

thus hid within the patient love of Christ,

Who fashions every moment of the day

of those who have a heart that longs to stay

and taste His proffered bread and waters sweet.

True nourishment to live awaited me.

The race of life is run on bended knee.

The Key

This key I hold so lightly in my hand.
Know I its great importance, or do I
so casually turn aside and lay it down
while prisoners of death pass me by?

Would I, had I the power to release,
not bend to help a sparrow in a snare?
And yet, I do withdraw God's offered peace
from souls who ride the storms of life's despair.

One turning of the key within the door
of one such seeking disenchanted heart,
Might be the instrument God doth employ
to thus unlock, His mercy to impart.

To bind or loose within my power to give.
Will I withhold the Word that sets men free?
This Word of Truth within me ever lives ~
Good News to all for all eternity.

Take up the key to heaven's vast domain.
Boldly go empowered by the Lord.
Seek every means to hallow Jesus' name
that He might enter every opened door.

A Disciple's Prayer

Dearest Jesus, draw us near.

Cause us e'er Your voice to hear.

Hold us safe within Your breast.

Only in You, are we blessed.

You are all our souls desire ~

We join the ever growing fire

To spread Your love throughout the earth...

May all we meet know their rebirth.

We'll sing Your everlasting song

And testify of You as long

As You are pleased to give us breath.

Oh, Gracious One, in You we rest.

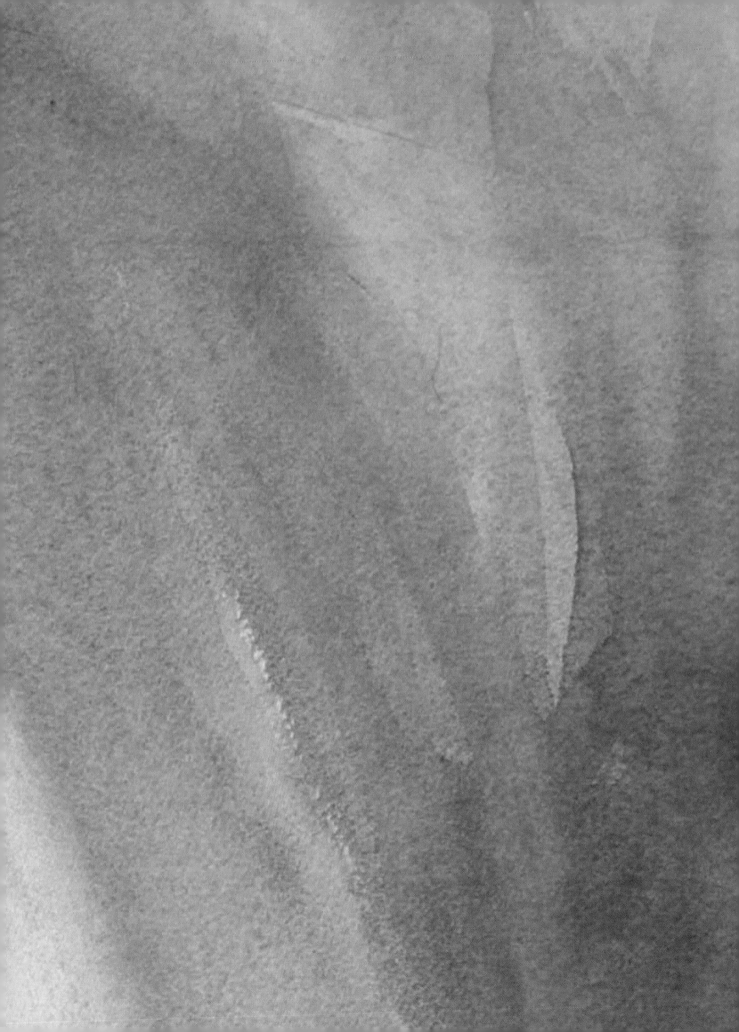

SPIRITUAL WARFARE

In conclusion, be strong in the Lord – be empowered through your union with Him; draw your strength from Him – that strength which His boundless might provides.

Put on God's whole armor – the armor of a heavy armed soldier which God provides – that you may be able successfully to stand up against all the strategies and the deceits of the devil.

EPHESIANS 6:10;11

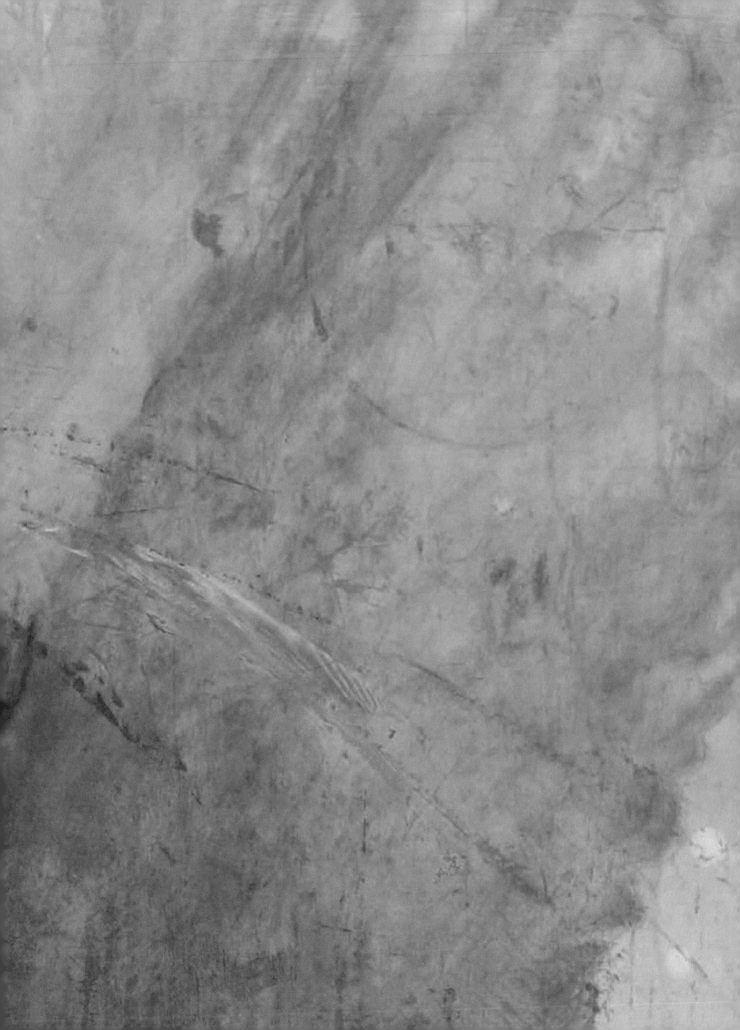

 Entering In

Have you entered into God's rest today,
and found that peace within;
or, does the battle in your heart
seem solely yours to win?
Have you trusted in His finished work,
or do you labor still
to gain the ground that seems so lost,
as you struggle with your will?

"The battle is Mine", saith the Lord,
"I have fought the enemy.
Do not strive so needlessly,
I have won the victory.
I am seated in the heavenlies,
resting, for you see,
My work has been completed,
and you're seated here with Me."

Let us strive to find that rest in Him
where fear cannot abide;
where enemies have been destroyed,
and can no longer chide;
where our faith is at its purest,
based solely on His power
to see us through our darkest night,
to strengthen us each hour.

Victory

Rise up, Oh King, inside of me.
Take Your place of authority.
Remand all foes that seek to steal,
to kill, destroy Your pleasant will
that rules within this frame of dust.
Rise up, Oh King, You must!

Take charge and now...yes, overthrow
all kingdoms banished to below.
This battlefront to You belongs.
Oh, wield Your mighty sword and strong.
All yield unto Your Word's command.
And in Your power, I stand.

Great God in heaven ~ on my side.
What enemy can dare to chide
and mock the Sovereign to His face
when I am armored in His grace.
Oh, weak, defeated, fiendish imp,
I laugh as you now from me limp!

On Dying to Self

Early awakening; sweetness holds
the musings of this sleep-refreshed soul.
Comforting thought: another night
arrested in God's peaceful care.
Open your eyes, if you dare.
The day awaits your solemn plight.

Another awakening, deep within,
boldly seeking this day to win;
to mold each action, each spoken word
of this unsuspecting, hapless lad,
while yet his sleepy eyes are clad
with visions of faithfully serving his Lord.

Eagerly, he seeks to still
this endless battle o'er his will.
The victory, he ever gains
within the veil, behind the cross,
where death holds pain but knows no loss;
yes, death to self and all its claims.

Arena of Grace

Accusing One, with loathsome fear,
you seek to cause dismay.
Maliciously, you hurl your spear
at me today.

You strut about, Purveyor of Doom,
to plan your every move.
Odiously, you taunt, you croon ~
my soul, reprove.

You burst upon my peaceful scene
confusion now to bring.
Cautiously, with stealth, you preen;
my guilt to sing.

If I did err to entertain
your charge but for a time,
sadistically, your vile disdain
would me entwine.

Oh, Lord of Unconditional Love,
defender for this hour,
make now this stage, arena of
Your glorious power.

My confidence must ne'er remain
within myself alone.
My Sovereign, only You can claim
this purchased throne.

Loneliness

Loneliness enwraps me as a shroud,
weaving webs of torturous deceit.
My silent tears I cannot cry aloud.
No one must know this tomb of my defeat.

With each new wrapping, darkness more obscures
the light of seeing each new day, a start.
And muffled sounds, without, as life endures
become a distant echo in my heart.

"Retreat!", the battle cry this tomb resounds.
"Hide within the safety of these walls.
Rejection, your periphery, surrounds.
Now seal the door of entrance to these halls."

Soon the comfort found within grows cold.
Rejection steals its slithering way inside.
Uselessness, now mine to have and hold.
Alas and from myself I cannot hide.

A voice arises from my dark despair,
echoing above, within, below.
With simple hope-filled words, "I hear, I care",
my Lord makes me His saving love to know.

His bright and glorious presence fills the tomb.
Rejection with its twin, Self-pity, flee.
Loneliness, displaced for lack of room
can no more bind my soul. I am set free!

 *Saving Grace*

Where is my heart? What passion strong,
save God, do I yet fondly seek?
What stronghold does the enemy
still maintain? Lord, where am I weak?

'Tis only as Your loving hand
places me in direst straits
that all that wills except Your will
can surface. Grace then overtakes.

On each occasion that I find
my self not equal to the task,
while sinking, I can call Your name,
"Lord, save me!" I need only ask.

Why did I think, as babe in You,
a pinnacle of sin erased
could here on earth be realized
with no more need of seas of grace?

As if this little fish could grow
and venture out upon its own
to swim the distance for Your sake
in harmful waters, depths unknown.

The lure of sin, its tentacles,
so wickedly the heart entwines
deceiving even best of men.
No one escapes its awful tines.

Where is my heart? Lord, Thou dost know
its passions all. I must not fret
but freely swim in saving grace,
schooled and safe within Your net.

Trusting

With a quiet, trusting heart
I walk in the heritage of Christ my King
Who by His own atoning blood
purchased for me, everything
pertaining to life for eternity.
I, in Him and He, in me.

With a longing, hope-filled soul
I rest in Jesus' glorious grace
Who gives His beloved in her sleep
blessings, sweet blessings all her days.
Awaken, my heart, to believe.
All of Christ, I receive.

With a powerless human strength
I lay down my weapons that cannot prevail
and put on the armor of my God
Who shields my soul within the veil.
I drink in the Spirit of my Lord
Who performs for me His faithful Word.

The Flesh and The Spirit

In the weakness of my flesh,
I cannot count all things as loss,
nor offer up to You my life
to let Your fire burn the dross.
Yet in my heart I long to know
the sweetness only of Your face ~
to have You mold Your life within
this wretchedness, that, by Your grace,
I might consent to watch and pray,
obeying Love's succinct command.
And, in the face of darkness here,
find empowerment to stand.
Oh, willing Spirit, strengthen me.
Overthrow my fleshly bent.
Seize my mind, my soul, my will.
Let my life, for Christ, be spent.

 Consumed

Lord, by Thy love I am consumed.
Before Thy gaze I melt
until my shame can find no room ~
a child who knows no guilt.

For this brief moment I enjoy
the freedom of Your grace.
Its legal tender, I employ
and all is hope and peace.

Could I but stay and rest a while
and relish Your delight.
Your warm embrace, Your tender smile
bring comfort day and night.

But, how my mind doth torture me
with worldly thought and care
that crowd into Eternity
where You await me there.

Pray! I quickly tell my heart
and fervently I cry,
"Lord, rid the beast...make him depart
with every fear and lie."

My anxious heart, I bring to You
Who only can relieve.
This battleground cannot undo
Your blood bought victory.

Oh, for the day I will away...
consumed, no more to long.
This devil world will never sway
me from my Easter song.

Grace

Grace washes

over me ~

a warm

liquid of the

love of God ~

enveloping,

penetrating,

permeating,

leaving in

its flow the

all~embracing

peace that,

just as I am,

I am loved

and accepted

by Holy God,

Who is Love.

No struggle

to perform.

No labor.

None of me.

All of Christ.

He is enough.

I receive.

XI

OUR ETERNAL HOME

Do not let your hearts be troubled. You believe in and adhere to and trust in and rely on God, believe in and adhere to and trust in and rely also on Me.

In My Father's house there are many dwelling places. If it were not so, I would have told you, for I am going away to prepare a place for you. And when I go and make ready a place for you, I will come back again and will take you to Myself, that where I am you may be also.

JOHN 14:1-3

One

Oh! Blissful day
when I will meet
my precious Lord ~
communion sweet.
This veil of flesh
He will remove.
Nothing between
to hinder love.
Consummation!
Yearning no more.
Eternity
ours to enjoy.
All is known.
We are one.

Eternal Hope

Now You lay me down to sleep,

Eternal Son, my soul to keep.

Though, in the world, I no more wake,

I thank You, Lord, my soul You take

to be with You forevermore,

to praise, to worship, and adore.

I gaze into Your loving eyes,

my soul rejoices, as it cries,

in gratitude for Calvary,

"Oh, Master, Savior, Lord to me!"

And, on that day, when trumpets sound,

and angels gather all around,

I will meet you in the air,

my body raised, so to declare,

"Holy, precious Jesus be

now fully glorified in me."

Lord, I Come

Grieve not for me as one who has no hope.
Comfort one another with this word...
Death, once feared, but now defeated foe
has ushered me into the arms of God.

Even now, I'm present with our Christ,
Who rules in majesty upon His throne.
He welcomes me, His child, with sheer delight.
All kingdom mysteries, He now makes known.

Lovely, oh so lovely is the Lamb.
Alas, and with what joy the Father gives
all glory, honor, might into His hand
and grants me, by His grace, to ever live.

Most Benevolent Father, Faithful Son,
Blessed Sacred Spirit - Three in One,
I bow before Your holy, all shekinah glory.
In gratitude, with humble heart, I come.

The Parting

There is a tie that runs so deep

that one is unaware of its strength

till destiny forces a wide dry gulf

of separation...enough

to stretch the heart in anguished longing

as memories unleash their haunting

pictures of a pleasant past.

Projection toward the future casts

a steely gray and empty dawn

as the chasm opens in a yawn.

There stands the heart, torn and bleeding...

pure love sore manifest in the parting.

Hope in Grief

Dear Lord,

Give unto me Your joy.

My joy is ever fleeting.

Grace me with Your power.

My strength doth wain, receeding.

The hour has come...more to be done.

Now grief must cease its pleading.

Rest, my beloved, rest,

in arms of peace, awaiting.

In Christ, our life is hid

together, ever sating.

I must go on until the Son

fain beckons, ne'er delaying.

Then joy complete is known.

Forever we are One...

True Life never ceasing.

Face to Face

Face to face, I long to be
to truly know God's love for me.
Great mystery to be revealed
as I approach fair Zion's hill.
All knowledge then will be replaced
by Truth etched in my Savior's face.
All faith, all hope then realized
while gazing in His loving eyes.
Oh, keep me, Spirit, till that day
perfection comes and then away
with all that now doth hinder me
and holds me bound. I shall be free!

Heaven

To fully experience the glory that is God.

To be taken up into Divine Goodness, Holiness, and Perfect Love...

Abandoned to His pleasure, well pleased to do His bidding.

Fully revealed, nothing hidden.

The ache, the longing at last fulfilled.

Uniqueness perfected, not abandoned, invoking the smile of God.

Harmony, bliss, peace, joy.

Truly knowing what I was made for.

A perfect fit ~ welcomed home by the One, Christ Jesus,

Who went before to prepare a place for me,

And prepared me for the place called

Heaven.

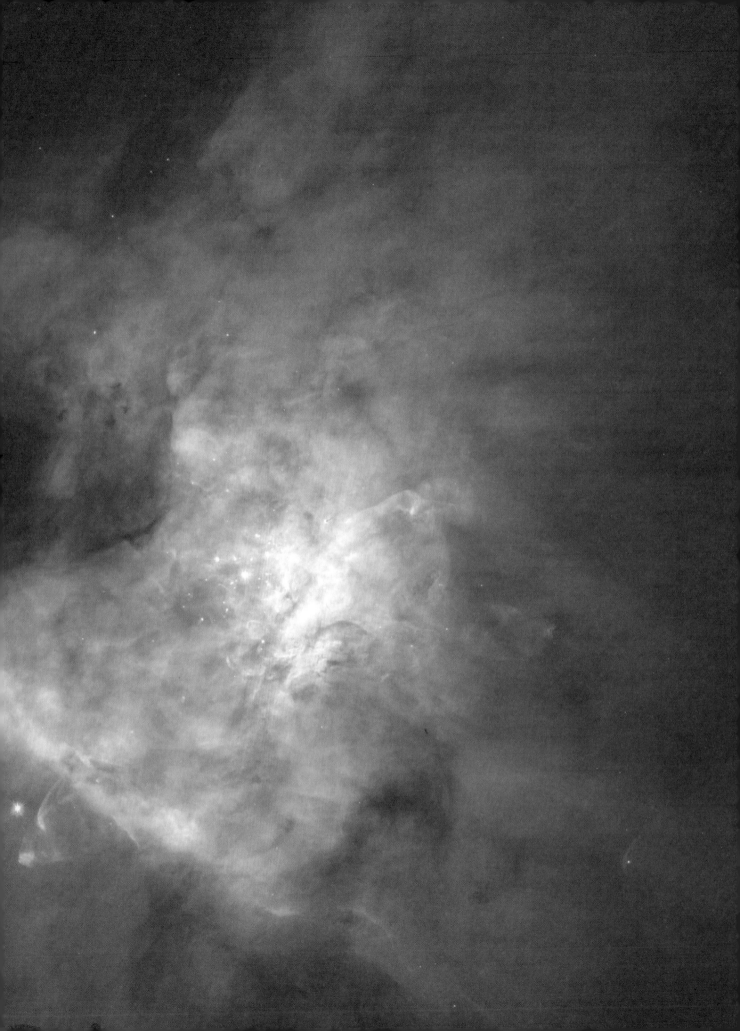

XII

BREATH OF HEAVEN

Breath of Heaven

I
THE CREATION

God breathes, "Let there be...", and worlds exist;

a whisper only, and seas gather to reveal dry land;

a shout!, and stars explode in the firmament.

God bends and gathers dust of earth to mold His image.

Oh, Breath of Life, filling newly-formed lungs:

first man--first man-breath:

A cry to heaven!...

inexpressible joy: man face to face with his creator,

breathing His breath, freely, in total innocence.

And life is sweetly sustained in the garden called Eden...

peace...love...joy...rest...

II
THE FALL

Words of cunning and deceit breathed into man's ear;

temptation as a subtle breeze becomes a howling wind,

until man bows his heart to another god,

and breathes innocent breath no more.

And in that once delight-filled garden, God whispers, "Where are

you?"

No cry of joy...

only timid speech laced with guilt.

Oh, labored breath--running, hiding, toiling,

searching......searching...

III
THE NATIVITY

Star-filled sky looking down upon a stable obscure,

known only by the expectant two and the few

guided there by Sovereignty.

Oh, sound beloved to a mother's ear:

the infant Jesus gasps, and breates the first man-breath of God.

Cry of Heaven!...

God descending, breathing new life into His world.

Innocent breath once more filling a man-child;

and the worlds created by His own breath

break forth into rejoicing over His coming.

And Mary, face to face with her tiny bundle,

breathing the sweet breath of her creator,

rejoices quietly in her heart, knowing not

the many tears she would shed for her son,

nor the grief He would bear for mankind.

But for now there is peace....peace...

IV
THE PASSION

A quiet garden for prevailing prayer;

the battleground for all humanity.

Tears mingle with drops of sweat as blood,

as the God-man breathes the scent of that bitter cup.

Cry of Heaven to Heaven!...

then total submission to the Sovereign will.

The battle, raged and won, in Gethsemane, while just outside

mankind breathes quietly in his sleep-filled darkness, unaware.

sleep....sleep...

V
THE CRUCIFICTION

Awake!, to see your leader scorned!

Words of derision breathed into His ear.

Shouts of anger over His bold claims.

Labored breath in His still innocent lungs,

bearing the beam that will hold His last breath.

Tears of agony flowing down that awful beam

mingle with tears of those He called His own.

A cry to Heaven...why?...why?..,

as innocence becomes both sin and sacrifice.

Then God breathes a last man-breath;

and the silence is deafening.

.....

VI
THE ATONING

Then heaven holds its sacred breath,

while darkness blanketeth the skies.

A few of mankind cry with grief,

while others breathe sighs of relief;

but, most go unaffected through their day.

And earth awaits the thunderous swell...

await....await...

VII
THE RESURRECTION AND ASCENSION

Oh, resurrection Breath of God
breathed into sacred lungs once more!
Cry of Heaven's victory!...
o'er death and all opposing foes.
Arise, arise, oh Lamb of God!
Breathe breath of joy's eternity,
and go to take Your rightful place
beside Your Father, face to face.
Rejoice!...Rejoice!...Rejoice!...

VIII
THE PENTACOST

Holy Spirit, sent from Heaven's throne.

Like a wind: mighty, Nordic, rushing;

then gentle as the tropic breezes.

Heaven's spotlight: bright, raw, exposing;

then softly lighting pathway toward redemption.

A cry to Heaven!...

man-tears of pain o'er guilt, pleading forgiveness.

Christ's own life breathed into souls thus yielded;

and innocence once sought by ever running,

Let everything that has breath and every breath of life praise the Lord.

Praise you the Lord!

Hallelujah!

PSALM 150:6

ACKNOWLEDGEMENTS

To **Judy Durham**, my special friend for fifty years. Thank you for your love and encouragement over our lifetime; and for introducing me to the amazing works of the Holy Spirit of God. You have been my spiritual mentor and true friend.

To **Suzy Schultz**, inspired artist, whose beautiful works grace the pages of this book. I first saw her artistry many years ago and had a dream to collaborate with her on a book of my poetry. Dreams really do come true when they are birthed in the Lord. Thank you, Suzy. *You can see more of her work at www.suzyschultz.net*

To **Amy Jo Sledge**, graphic designer, who designed this book so creatively.

ABOUT THE AUTHOR

Jenny Mathews was born Frances Virginia Lee in Atlanta, Georgia, where she resided most of her life. She graduated from Georgia State University with a BA in mathematics. She married Dwight Mathews after graduating who was a CPA with Haskins and Sells...later to become Deloitte. Dwight passed in 2013. They had two children, Julie and Rich. She now resides in Winter Park, Florida near her daughter. She started writing poetry at age thirty. This book is a compilation of these poems, which represents her spiritual journey over forty years. In the fall of 2017, she felt it was time to begin the process of publishing her life's work of writing.